CHOICE AND ADAPTATION OF TECHNOLOGY IN DEVELOPING COUNTRIES

An Overview of Major Policy Issues

*Review of the discussions held
at the study sessions organised
by the OECD Development Centre,
Paris, 7th-9th November, 1972*

DEVELOPMENT CENTRE
OF THE ORGANISATION
FOR ECONOMIC CO-OPERATION AND DEVELOPMENT
PARIS 1974

The opinions expressed and arguments employed in this publication
are the responsibility of the authors
and do not necessarily represent those of the OECD.

*
* *

TABLE OF CONTENTS

Part One

REVIEW OF DISCUSSIONS

by

Martin Brown and Mikoto Usui

Part Two

RAPPORTEURS' SUMMING UP AND WRITTEN SUBMISSIONS REVIEWING OR SUPPLEMENTING THE DISCUSSION

Part Three

SUMMARIES OF BACKGROUND PAPERS

PREFACE

A meeting on Choice and Adaptation of Technology in Developing Countries, organised by the OECD Development Centre, took place in Paris from 7th to 9th November 1972. It was participated in by some 50 people from various parts of the world, having different disciplinary backgrounds and occupations, but all eager to broaden their frontiers of communication on matters related to "technology and development". In fact, the title of the meeting was inviting discussions on both technical aspects of "appropriate technology" and the broader policy environments being challenged thereby. This made it desirable to let the forum move on in an almost "open-house" style. The very heterogeneity of participants could be, it was hoped, a test-stone of possibilities open for a comprehensive appraisal of technology policies for development in the developing countries.

The forum was tightly, and even tensely, packed throughout the three days. With no more than 18 hours shared by 50 participants, the actual discussions were inevitably fragmentary and inconclusive on the most important issues. However, the experiment has left a precious raw material to be worked on by the Development Centre as well as by individual participants. Given the complexity of the subject, it seemed appropriate for the Centre to undertake a further review of certain aspects of it, even drawing on the large amount of discussion going on elsewhere. In doing so, an attempt has been made to explore where we are with particular issues of technology for developing countries and what sort of lines of research seem to be most desirable at this stage.

And at this stage, the major outcome is represented by eleven short essays included in Part One of this document ("Review of Discussions"). Many of these essays often show the authors' own reflections on the issues relating to respective subjects. They refer sometimes to remarks and articles contributed by particular participants, and sometimes to other writers not directly involved in the meeting. Chapters I, IV and X were authored mainly by

Martin Brown, and Chapters II, III, V to IX by myself. Chapter XI
consists of an assembly, with only minor editing of the taped
discussions as they touched on questions of "information". The
earlier draft (issued as of March 1973 in a mimeographed form)
has been partially amended taking into account the comments and
suggestions received during the past months. The authors of Part
One are grateful for all those who were good enough to appear among
the dramatis personae in this (often aggressive) review. Merits of
these essays, if any, should be first credited to these people,
while the authors remain solely responsible for any errors and
insufficiencies committed in citation and interpretation.

Still another outcome is the set of statements and notes
contributed by individual participants after the meeting. These
are gathered in Part Two of this document. Due to the shortage of
time, the concluding session could afford to have only eight
speakers recapitulate individually what they themselves thought
had emerged as major issues and conclusions during the meeting.
The taped speeches were subsequently edited, amended and expanded
by the speakers themselves: they are Frances Stewart (U.K.),
Bepin Behari (India), Daniel Carrière (France), Nuno de Figueiredo
(Brazil), José Giral B. (Mexico), M.A.M. Shabaan (Egypt),
Simon Titel (Inter-American Development Bank) and Joseph E. Stepanek
(UNIDO). Several other participants, who wished to supplement those
statements but could not do so at the meeting, kindly supplied the
Centre with their written notes. They are: Peter Harper (U.K.).
Dennis Goulet (U.S.A.), Jacques de Bandt (France), Jacques Perrin
(France), Hans A. Havemann (Germany) and P.C. Trussell (WAITRO).

In contrast to those two Parts which present the reviews and
reflections obtained after the meeting, Part Three refers solely
to what the various participants brought with them before the
meeting. There were nearly forty background papers (see the list
in the Annex) submitted by them, mostly on their own initiative.
Many of these papers were referred to during the discussions, but
this collection occurred without the Centre's systematic planning
in terms of their orientations and content. To do justice to this
characteristic of the meeting, (and owing to the limited space
available for this publication), only summaries or excerpts of
about 20 privately submitted papers are included here. Other
reference materials, mostly authored institutionally, such as those
brought in by OAS, UNIDO, and U.S. Department of State are omitted
even though some of them actually offered an important basis for
the discussion. These summaries were made by the Development Centre

staff and checked by respective authors. Nothing would better
convey the merits of these contributions than their original
texts. Assuming that there will be other places and opportunities
for publication in their full forms, we hope that these summaries,
when taken as a whole, will adequately meet the purpose of this
particular document. Work related to this Part was shared mainly
by Antonio Dos Santos and Guy Crespin who also took part in the
production of the French version of the entire text.

Mikoto Usui
Head,
Technology and Industrialisation
Programme,
OECD Development Centre.

June 1973.

Part One

<u>REVIEW OF DISCUSSION</u>

by

Martin Brown and Mikoto Usui

SUMMARY OF CONCLUSIONS

The diversity of opinion which emerged at the meeting reflected basically a range of views as to the nature of the problems. Overlapping this was another dimension of differences in view, as to whether the purpose of the discussions was primarily about research or about action. Further, the forum brought together people with different professional interests and roles in relation to the subject. On the part of the organiser, the Development Centre of the OECD, there was in fact stronger interest in comprehending the pattern of divergence being displayed than in reiterating the least vulnerable kind of generalisations that people already tended to produce elsewhere on the subject. Indeed it was because of this view that we adopted the procedure of having a closing session devoted to summing up by individual rapporteurs, each person to his own taste. These individual attempts to summarise conclusions, reproduced in Part Two, will convey most of the differing viewpoints. In this section we merely attempt to give a sample of discussions that seem particularly important in comprehending the overall configuration of various issues.

Terminology and Underlying Policy Issues (Chapter I and Part Two)

There was no agreement on what words to use or on whether it matters what words are used. Some participants felt that discussion of terminology was a waste of time, because one could separate the real issues from the terminology. Others argued that terminology is not neutral and may frequently influence our thinking and action.

There was considerable agreement that there is a mutual interaction between:

a) technology choice and technology adaptation;
b) employment, income distribution and consumption patterns;
c) industrial structure and factor prices; and
d) social organisation and political structures.

But there were wide differences in views on the extent to which technology issues can be handled separately at different levels of policy making, planning and decision taking.

The Role of Factor Prices (Chapters II and V)

Nobody doubted that LDC market prices diverge widely from social opportunity costs. The problem was to determine how relevant this is to technology choice, and what should be done about it. Some argued insistently that frequently (e.g. in textiles) the wrong technology is chosen because of factor price distortions. Others argued that factor price distortions need to be related to the whole complex of issues about industrialisation strategy, industrial dualism, foreign investments, capacity of development administration, "engineering man" in the privileged, monopolist sector, etc. These relevant basic issues could lead us well beyond the mere question of reform of fiscal incentive schemes.

Industrial Dualism and the Unprivileged Sector (Chapters II and V)

Technology problems clearly differ between the large scale modern sector and the rest of an LDC economy. The technology system in the latter sector seems often such that there is economically greater scope for use of capital than for use of additional labour. But incentives for implantation of foreign technology do not easily coincide with incentives for adaptive innovations on indigenous technology. There was no agreement on the extent to which – for technological or growth reasons – the modern sector should be promoted, nor agreement on the extent to which its promotion would be to the detriment of less privileged sectors. One has to know more about the ways these sectors respond to the entire policy environments and their ramifications in terms of economic, social and institutional measures which affect the diffusion of technology in these sectors.

Sectoral Problems (Part Three, b)

There was some discussion of individual industrial sector problems based on participants' presentation of case studies. It was clear that the different sectors present very different technology problems, but the discussion was not sufficiently detailed or extensive to allow more informative conclusions.

Soft or Alternative Technology (Chapter I, Part Two, especially Harper)

Participants showed surprising enthusiasm for the promotion of radical technology experiments, which would correspond to radical views about the physical and social environment and about social and political organisation. There was little discussion about how this should co-exist with more conventional technology; some felt that soft technology was merely at one end of a spectrum of technologies, a technology for the least privileged of the unprivileged sectors. Others linked it with the Chinese technology policy for local industrialisation. On reflection, however, such impressions might be said to be somewhat off-line. It remains to be seen how far the groping of soft technologists in a post-industrialisation society can bear upon technology policies for a pre-industrialisation society.

The Price of Technology Transfer (Chapter IV, Parts Two and Three)

There was general agreement that the cost of technology transferred to LDCs is sometimes excessive, and that LDCs could give some priority to reducing such costs. There was, however, no agreement on the criteria for determining an appropriate cost for particular transfers of technology, or on how important the pricing problems are, or on what sorts of measures would be appropriate.

Some participants took the UNCTAD line on the identification of technology transfers costs, advocating the establishment by LDCs of national supervisory agencies and perhaps even an international brokerage ensuring acquisition and distribution for LDC local users at fair prices. Other participants felt that such ideas would just scratch the surface and that price questions were perhaps less important than questions of use and absorption capacity. Too low a transfer price for technology could possibly inhibit local adaptation.

Multinational Corporations (MNCs) (Chapter III)

Three broad issues seemed important about MNCs:

a) whether they perform better or worse than the alternatives in adapting technology to LDC conditions, especially factor endowments;

b) whether they distort consumption patterns and the choice of products on offer in LDCs;

c) how well they promote (or inhibit) linkage effects within LDC economies and LDC capacities to innovate.

There was wide disagreement on the first issue, reflecting differing views about the capacity of different LDC institutions to absorb and neutralise such external forces and, more generally, about the orientation and strength of MNCs on the international scene. b) and c) appeared less debatable; MNCs certainly tend to create enclaves. Some even ventured to suggest that LDCs should totally close their doors to MNCs. Others favoured the stepping-up of international actions towards a "code of conduct". No one disagreed, however, about the infancy of empirical research on MNC behaviour.

Science and Industry (Chapter VI)

While science policy, R and D policies and educational policies are obviously relevant to technology choice and adaptation, the practical institutional implications are far-reaching. The problem of establishing an effective dialogue between scientist, technologist, politicians, planners, economists and others has proved quite intractable in many developed countries. LDCs may have less vested interests - competing science institutions of different vintages - and, therefore, perhaps more flexibility towards the specific goal-conscious approach. If this relieves them of some of the intractabilities in one order of decision problems, (i.e. those concerned with the choice and design of policy-implementing institutions), another order of technology policy decision that concerns the choice of appropriate technologies may remain less tractable in LDCs to the extent that it tends to be bi-modal: i.e. to catch up with modern technological advancement on the one hand, and to create more employment on the other. Moreover, LDC technology "needs" are enormous compared to their meagre resources. And most of the linkage problems (e.g. industry-university links) should be an immediate object of institutional policy design and not just a matter of occasional "nudging".

Technology Assessment (Chapter VII)

As its French translation (la maitrise de la technologie) implies, technology assessment represents the newly emerging effort to grip "technology" as an object of direct policy control at the governmental level. This effort is characterised by the

research for an evaluation method based on multi-dimensional
criteria, instead of the conventional approach of the single-
numeraire type. When applied to a relatively short-term situation
in an LDC, such as decisions on manufacturing plants to be imported,
there would be a fear that too serious an assessment effort might
result in "technology arrestment". Apparently, the kind of exercise
actually being made in the DC context of environmental policies
do not seem to match closely the LDC preoccupations about technology choice and adaptation. However, real choices are in fact
open at a number of different levels of policy decision. This
demands a serious review of the available "system" alternatives,
ranging from the macro-strategy level to the micro-product - and
process-engineering level - a challenge to the conventional single-
numeraire growth concept, in favour of a broader, and more incisive
framework of policy appraisal for "technology and development".

"Modules" of Industrial Technology (Chapter IX)

Apart from the question of the tractability of "technology"
at a macro-strategy level, which is not yet very far removed from
philosophical debates, technology in practice seems tractable only
at certain levels of specificity. Identification of alternatives
open for choice and possibilities for adaptation would not go very
far unless given packages of technology could be broken down into
various components or modules; and in so doing, one ought to go
beyond those best-practised technologies on the shelf, giving open-
minded reconsideration to discarded laboratory results, as well as
to technologies now considered obsolete by today's major industrial
concerns. Quite a few exercises exist showing that there are in
fact hundreds of alternative process design possibilities for a
given product line, even in industries with relatively continuous
processes. An information-intensive and brain-intensive "unpacking"
effort could thus rediscover nearly continuous stretches of the
neo-classical economist's iso-quant. It appears that the concept
of "modules", which facilitates such unpacking and innovative
adaptation of industrial technology, deserves further exploration
for the benefit of R and D planning and related information service
policy in LDCs.

Engineering Consultancy (Chapter X)

Most participants agreed that "engineering" is a focal point
at which knowledge from different sources comes together to shape

the design of projects, and often even the planning of industrial
sectors. Engineering consultancy institutions play an important
role in the technology transfer process in LDCs. But there was
considerable disagreement as to the organisational and policy
implications of this role.

Some argued that DC engineering contractors are necessarily
dependent on process licensors and equipment manufacturers; they
only promote the integration of LDC industries into DC markets
and thus strengthen the technological dependency of LDCs. To break
this dependency, LDCs must endeavour to develop their own engineering capabilities. That much was a logically clear conclusion, but
its institutional implications were not straightforward. Other
participants associated the subject matter with a broader range
of consultant agencies of which engineering contractors constitute
only a part. The involvement of these agencies in consultancy on
pre-investment decisions (where in fact more important choice
situations appear to occur) points to the need for a more incisive
typology of consulting institutions.

As to possible institution-building strategies, there seem
to exist a host of questions that call for a better understanding
of the basic objectives and constraints: the evolution of consul-
tant-client relationships on a commercial basis; government-industry
interfaces that define the relevant institutional (and financial)
base for consultancy development; development of local capital-
goods producing industries viewed both as a major source of expertise and as clients; and so on. These seem to suggest an as yet
almost virgin territory for research, perhaps difficult to step
into, but important for over-all policy design for LDC technological development.

Information Services (Chapter XI)

There was general agreement on some general, not very practical, conclusions. However, there was clear and considerable disagreement on most practical conclusions. "Information services",
whether national or international, are obviously not the only
channel for technology diffusion. It is important to see how various
other relevant channels should relate to this particular one. Some
made a distinction between information which is public, and proprietary (or commercial) information to which access is at present
more or less controlled: more information should be (and can be)
shifted to the public category. Some participants stressed a
distinction between different uses for which information is needed.

At the project design level, much more detailed commercial information is required than at the sectoral planning level, and public
information services may be less well adapted to this role.

So there was, in practice, no concensus in favour of extension
or strengthening of official information services. Some argued
strongly that this was important, but others felt equally strongly
that the benefits would be partly illusory, to the extent that they
bounce away at the limit of local industrialists' capacity to
absorb and adapt technological information. The total policy design
to influence that limit could present less tractable, but equally
urgent, problems.

International Aid

Given their differing professional, geographical and political
standpoints, participants were inevitably in considerable disagreement about the possible role for foreign aid. There was an evident
lack of knowledge on the part of many participants about the mechan-
ics of present aid practices. On the present situation, many participants felt that soft capital aid helped distort LDC factor
prices, bolstered inappropriate LDC technology policies and reinforced commercial relations of technological dependency. Technical
assistance was also felt often to reinforce relations of dependency.

Apart from the general "aid-disillusionment", however, a
significant proportion of the participants were from donor agencies
preoccupied about how to design better aid programmes in the field
of science and technology. There was generally a strong forward
attitude prevailing among them, stemming from the realisation that
technology in the LDC development context is too complex to be
handled by the conventional instruments of development aid practised
so far; technology aid should be conceived, not just as one of the
numerous ways of filling LDC resource gaps, but as an attempt at
affecting more directly the development capability of LDC people.
This is not to suggest any short cut but, on the contrary, to
suggest looking at the whole complex of mechanisms, resources and
policies for technological development.

Chapter I

TERMINOLOGY AND UNDERLYING POLICY ISSUES

Some study group participants argued that there is no need
for a discussion of semantics. Such an argument could reflect
several rather different standpoints, with quite different
objectives. For example, one may be preoccupied by the need for
LDCs to use equipment appropriate to their factor endowments, by
the need to maximise the use of local materials, by the need to
maximise employment creation or by the need to install machinery
which can be used with engineering efficiency. Nevertheless one
might be able to establish and discuss such objectives and the
means of meeting them without needing any great discussion of the
terminology to be used. Alternatively, some participants felt that,
although there was need to distinguish clearly the words used by
different groups of people, discussions of terminology and philosophical issues tend to divert attention from practical issues
about how to promote a better use of technology in LDCs.

By contrast, some participants felt that, although discussions
of terminology may not always be satisfactory, there are problems
of semantics which need to be raised in the context of a general
discussion of objectives and issues. Most directly, this is because
different groups, who are operationally involved, in different ways,
have adopted labels (even slogans): these labels are inevitably
used in day-to-day activities without the supporting analysis
which identifies moré precisely their meaning. So, for example,
"intermediate technology" has come to be partly a label used to
refer to the sort of activity promoted by the Intermediate Technology Development Group. Less directly, expressions which have
been (sufficiently) clearly defined for use in one particular
context are carried over into much looser use in rather different
contexts.

One of the central problems about technology use in developing
countries is that issues are raised which seem to require the use
of language in relatively unusual ways. Most obviously, it seems

more urgent in developing countries than in developed countries
to have technology issues discussed by non-technologists. Much
greater emphasis is typically placed in developing countries on
national development planning and, more generally, on central
administrative intervention in industry: these activities have
been primarily conducted by general administrators. A second
(related) aspect seems to be that technology discussions may generally be less industry-specific in developing countries than in
developed countries. With the more complex industrial structures
of developed countries, discussions would more typically consist
of well-informed individuals discussing particular problems about
technical developments in particular industries. Moreover, much of
the general interest in "technology" for developing countries stems
from a belief that there are factors (within the developing economies or in relations between developed and developing economies)
which tend systematically to distort all choices involving technology. So, there is probably more looseness and confusion in
technology language when used in the LDC contexts than when used
in the developed countries, and therefore more need for discussion
of semantics.

The expression "appropriate technology" seems the most widely
favoured term, if only because it begs the important "questions".
But, by the same token, some dislike it. In its most normally used
sense, (some might say "in its correct logical use"), the expression
"appropriate" has empirical content only by reference to a particular situation involving the person who is using it. A technology
is only "appropriate" (or "inappropriate") by reference to criteria
or objectives which themselves must be specified in empirical terms.
There might, schematically, be two types of reason which made a
particular technology "inappropriate" for a particular situation.
The objectives being advocated might not be the most desirable
(or most appropriate), or, secondly, the technology employed might
not be consistent with reaching those objectives. The second type
of reason for "inappropriateness" should be an empirical matter.
By contrast, the logical status of objectives, and of their desirability or appropriateness, is very difficult to handle satisfactorily. However, in the unschematic, real world of development
planning and policy making it seems very difficult to identify and
handle "objectives" as value judgements separately from the methods
(e.g. technologies) proposed to meet those objectives.

So, the logic of the expression "appropriate" would allow two
speakers correctly to use the term "appropriate technology" to

refer to incompatible practical situations: their objectives
would be different. For example, the industrialisation and technology recommendations made for Algeria by a certain group of
advisors, involving for the moment a massive emphasis on capital-
intensive industry, must surely be incompatible with what, for
example, an advisory group from ITDG might recommend. Each group
might be logically correct in describing its own proposals as
involving an appropriate technology with reference to the particular objectives it stresses. More generally, a similar situation
may arise where partial objectives may be established for different sectors of an economy. The following Chapter discusses some
of the underlying problems of one fairly extreme possibility, the
so-called "dualistic economy". It is possible that one could have
consistent national objectives which involved e.g. international
free trade criteria, infant industry protection criteria and
employment-creation criteria, respectively, for three different
sectors. It is even possible that in some economies it would be
"appropriate" simultaneously to introduce radically different
technologies within the same industry. So, the expression "appropriate technology" becomes difficult to use in practice unless
the context and the objectives are adequately specified.

Three further points may be noted. First, the types of
"objectives" or "criteria" implied in most discussions about
technology use in LDCs are not specific enough to eliminate all
the available alternatives: there may frequently be alternative
appropriate technologies. By contrast, however, the objectives
might be overspecified, with the result that no option seems
"really appropriate" although some will be "less inappropriate"
than others. Thirdly, (as Frances Stewart has argued) an appropriate technology need not be the "optimum technology". The
optimum technology might require further application of existing
knowledge and experience to adaptation of the presently available,
"appropriate" technologies. Here again one is in empirical difficulty because, unless one adopts a very restrictive definition of
"existing knowledge and experience", one is not at all sure what
to regard as possible improvements on present appropriate technologies. Clearly, there is a central problem about the relevant
time-span within which possible developments are considered.

The Study Group discussions seemed to reflect a considerable
looseness in the use of the term "technology" at different times.
This is inevitable. By implication, there was no agreement as to
whether the term is in need of further logical analysis and

definition, and, if so, whether one should prefer a relatively restrictive or a relatively loose definition.

Frances Stewart's paper(1) cites the definitions suggested by Galbraith ("the systematic application of scientific and other organised knowledge to practical tasks")(2) and Baranson ("product design, production techniques and managerial systems to organise and carry out production plans")(3). She herself opts for a very loose definition, which she describes as follows: "Methods of production perhaps better describes the questions at issue. I shall take the technology adopted to mean everything concerned with and arising from production in the economy. With this very broad definition the appropriate technology amounts to the best way of organising production in an economy. This will be a function of the following four sets of variables:

i) the initial and historically determined way in which production is in fact organised

ii) different possibilities available in the current state of knowledge, including:

- idea for technique conceived;
- technique developed into prototype;
- technique applied commercially;
- technique produced on a commercial scale;
- technique adopted broadly in the country where it originated.

These five stages may all occur in a single country - the country where the idea originated. Before the technique is available, in a second country, knowledge about its availability and performance, and possibly also experience is required. Before it represents a real choice to all entrepreneurs in the second country therefore the following stages must be added:

- knowledge about technique transmitted to some entrepreneurs in a country where it did not originate;

1) "Intermediate Technology: A Definitional Discussion", (Background paper No.11).
2) The New Industrial Estate, Hamish Hamilton, 1967, p.12.
3) Industrial Technologies for Developing Economies, Praeger, 1969.

- technique imported and adopted by some entrepreneurs
   in some country which others may observe and subsequently copy.

iii) the resources available to the society;

iv) the aims of economic policy.

These four variables are interconnected in a number of ways.
The initial conditions are a product of past resources and a
determinant of current resources available. "The resources available, the initial conditions and the range of possibilties help
determine (but do not totally determine) the aims of economic
policy." Thus, Stewart notes, with such a wide definition "the
meaning of the same technology or '_the_ appropriate technology'
becomes ambiguous since there are so many ways in which methods
of production may differ."

Such a loose type of definition might appeal mainly, perhaps,
to economists and other social scientists. It would be generally
less useful, however, in the context of discussions among engineers
and technologists, or discussions about information systems. One
noticed that different concepts were being used by different
speakers during the Study Group discussions.

Some participants wondered whether underlying policy issues
have much relevance to most questions about appropriate technology.
One might argue that at the level at which technology decisions
are made (normally the plant/project level) the underlying policy
issues about development strategy are largely irrelevant. The
economic environment in which the project will actually have to
live is already relatively determined. The project's promotors
cannot normally influence greatly either the pattern of demand
for its products or the conditions under which it acquires (and
uses) capital equipment and current inputs and the prices it pays
for them. Moreover, some would argue that, at the project/plant
level, there is (in many situations) a real trade-off between
"efficiency" and "innovative adaptation" of technology. So, at
the plant/project level, not only may the scope for technology
adaptation, in practice be generally small, but also there may
frequently seem to be real economic penalties in the possible
adaptations. This sentiment, explicitly expressed by at least one
participant, would perhaps be challenged by most people. Obviously,
it is not meant to imply that the technology employed would be the
same with different national economic or social objectives. It is

rather that the process of implementing such different national
objectives would generally influence technologies employed in
more indirect and diffused ways - for example, through the structure of demand, through a different structure of actual factor
prices, through regional industrialisation or through fiscal and
exchange rate policies. The technology adaptation response would
be indirect, diffused and perhaps, gradual. One direct adaptation,
which would be observable at the aggregate level but which might
be irrelevant at the project level, would be the total (or partial)
elimination of certain industrial activities (or the introduction
of completely new activities). Thus the aggregate composition of
technology employed could shift (even dramatically) without any
conscious consideration of national policy objectives in relation
to appropriate technology choices at the project level. To some
extent, this argument applies also to appropriate technology consideration at the sector or national planning level.

The technology employed by a particular industry (and therefore in aggregate by the whole economy) is clearly partly determined by the pattern of products produced. A different balance of
products has different implications for the scale and organisation
of particular industries and for the equipment employed. The pattern
of products produced and consumed is partly determined by the level
and structure of incomes and partly by the structure of relative
product prices in the economy. (Let us set aside for the moment
the question of international trade and the structure of international prices.) The level and structure of incomes is partly
determined by government economic policies and, importantly, the
policies concerning the overall balance between industry, agriculture, service sectors, etc., may have a direct influence on the
structure of incomes. (Incidentally, this influence is not yet
adequately researched even in developed countries. The Development
Centre is currently conducting a case study on Greece.)

There is an element of circularity. The level and structure
of incomes affect the factor prices, as well as the pattern of
product demand, which affect decisions about the choice of technology, which in turn affect the structure of incomes and thus the
pattern of demand for products. So, decisions about technology
could reinforce themselves through incomes and consumer demand.
But the circularity starting from technology has in fact a number
of ramifications leading to various sub-loops of feed-forward and
feed-back, which individually present themselves for different
types of policy consideration. Policies which act directly on

income distribution (e.g. personal income tax) or on the pattern of consumer demand (e.g. indirect taxation) affect the technology which seems required, be it at the stage of producing consumer goods or at the stages of capital and intermediate goods. Some Study Group participants clearly felt that it was very important to act directly on the pattern of product demand and the distribution of income, while allowing technology to be determined primarily at the plant level - in response to the effects of other policies on the pattern of products "demanded".

One of the important ramifications spreads onto questions concerning the relations of an individual LDC economy with the rest of the world. To the extent that goods and services are "tradeable", import and export possibilities affect the appropriate choice of technology - on condition that domestic prices are adjusted to international prices. On the other hand, international trade between developed and less developed countries may create (or reinforce) relations of dependency (e.g. through the ownership of technology). Study Group participants reflected a wide range of views on the role of international trade and international prices. At one extreme were some who believed that integration into the world economy must generally be good. At the other extreme were those who were extremely preoccupied by the relations of dependency between unequal partners. Both groups would accept that if there is an important "dependency" danger, one must either seek to avoid it or must combat it by adequate technical competence and experience. One group holds that, in general, the best way to acquire such competence and experience is through promoting international trade, and that in most LDC contexts the dependency dangers can adequately be met by a combination of policy instruments which do not involve major direct interventions in international trade or major distortions between domestic and international prices. At the other extreme are those who argue that dependency relations are so prevalent and so intractible (between unequal partners) as to require important direct administrative action to restrict the scope of international economic relations. This group, for example, have strong reservations about the possible benefits of international subcontracting and are deeply suspicious of the role of multinational corporations and of present international engineering consultancy services. There was very little direct confrontation between these widely conflicting standpoints at the November Study Group.

Even at this end of the spectrum, however, there seems to be a great deal of hesitancy to resort to a radical isolationist

position. One may, perhaps seek to isolate certain sectors of an
LDC economy completely from the world economy. Some participants
were close to arguing that whatever could be produced locally
should be produced locally, in an economy with unemployed resources
and a balance-of-payments constraint. This argument seems to represent the activist position towards "self-help" in rural industrialisation. There, one hears more about the notion of "mission" (as
stressed by K.L. Nanjappa, Bepin Behari, Norton Young, etc.) than
about the macro economist's concern about the rate of growth,
saving gaps, inter-industry balances, investment gestation, etc.
Frances Stewart attempts to settle the economic question of efficiency for the "intermediate technology" movement in the traditional
sector by pointing to the need for new technology and investment
that would reduce the capital-output ratio while increasing the
capital-labour ratio. But how much investment would be required in
the production of such indigenous technological (and perhaps also
social) innovations is an empirical question that no one is yet
quite ready to answer. For the success of the intermediate/con-
venient technology missions, beyond their current significance as
isolated pilot projects, what sort of "scale" effects should be
envisaged and how should it affect the nation-state decisions of
today about overall resource allocation priorities? At a further
extreme of the spectrum looms the so-called "soft-technology". As
Peter Harper writes on it in a separate section of this document(1),
the terminology is still "half-baked", and often explained by
freely referring to a mixture of various elements of "alternative"
technologies. These "alternative" technologies reflect preoccupations about the physical environment, about ecology, about resource
conservation, about human-social relations, etc. One might say that
the exponents of soft technology are concerned to minimise the
risks in relation to a number of environmental dangers. For some
exponents these environmental risks include - perhaps as the main
element - risks in relation to the human environment. Modern industry and modern agriculture tend to bring forms of social relationship and social organisation which certainly undermine the traditional LDC social relationships, but which may also be held to be
more positively dehumanising. Thus, soft technology (or at least
some of those who speak of it) seems to incorporate some special
ideas about regional self-sufficiency and self-help.

---

1) Part Two, II,1, page 63.

Partly (but not perhaps exclusively) because of their radical assessment of the risks to the physical and human environment, the soft technology exponents seem to be more or less revolutionary. Some have drifted towards believing in small self-sufficient units because they judge that the conventional concept of modern society is inevitably breaking down under the weight of internal contradictions. There is a still more radical, philosophically relativist strand, which says that (perhaps only in our crisis situation) society should not organise the lives of individuals more than to a minimum degree. Upon that score, soft technology appears to represent even an anti-thesis to the recent movement along the lines of "technology assessment" (which is also briefly reviewed in a separate section later[1]. To the extent that it constitutes primarily a psychological reaction to the distasteful features of the current emphasis on growth, the destination of this trend is very difficult to evaluate. While most people believe in popular participation and self-help as positive forces in development, few are sufficiently decentralising to suggest abandoning most of the functions of a modern state. Indeed, perhaps paradoxically, some of the radical critics of orthodox development strategies for LDCs tend to be proponents of even stronger nationalist states. It is particularly difficult to relate this type of issue to technological considerations exclusively. Even if one rejected all large-scale industrial (or other) activities in favour of small-scale or "intermediate" technology problems, it would be naive to suppose that technical information and know-how, which call for a well-developed administrative apparatus, were not critically important.

In fairness to soft technologists in general, however, one must admit that they have no logical requirement to demonstrate that their ideas could be universally applied nor to show that even partial generalisation of their ideas (e.g. in a rural region) would be inconsistent with continued improvement on hard technology elsewhere. One would like to be able to think about costs and benefits in specifically identifiable terms, quantitative or qualitative. Indeed, soft technologists are inclined to count as benefits the absence or reduction of disagreeable features of present technology and the fact that people may be happier or more convivial working just as much but in a different technological environment. They are also inclined to argue that a different technological environment would release (or make possible the utilisation of) human

---

1) Part One, VII, page 63.

resources which could substitute to some extent for capital or
foreign exchange. Importantly, such arguments are not new and are
not at all confined to a far-out fringe of radical sociologists
and economists. One can try to some extent to bring such arguments
back into the mainstream of applied economic analysis by assigning
values to these costs and benefits which do not have market prices.
This may seem useful in limited situations, where, for example, a
particular soft technology experiment is being compared with a
more conventional project. In this way, one retains at least the
idea of an objective welfare function which one is seeking to
maximise. One could accept a limited number of non-economic constraints. However, is it a question of credibility that is at
stake? First, the soft technologists may have no wish to be put
back into traditional neo-classical economics or in the administrative structure of project planning which has developed alongside
it. Second, one unresolved problem is to assess how far the idea
of economic maximisation can be successfully translated into
development planning and policy in a context that emphasises grass-
roots participation and local initiative.

Chapter II

SUCCESSES IN THE UNPRIVILEGED SECTOR:
WHAT IS THERE TO BE TRANSFERRED?

As Ul Haq of IBRD remarked in commenting on Gustav Ranis'
article on "the economic framework for optimum LDC utilisation
of technology"(1), we spent many years thinking of development
strategy in terms of the Arthus Lewis two-sector model. According
to that model, development is defined as a uni-directional process
whereby the traditional sector is gradually absorbed by the modern
sector. In international forums for transfer of technology (such
as that of UNCTAD), too, we still hear the familiar term, "income

---

1) Technology and Economics in International Development, Report
   of the Seminar held in Washington D.C. on 23rd May, 1972,
   US AID Office of Science and Technology (TA/OST 72-9), p.41.

gap" between LDCs and DCs, and the "technology gap" that underlies it; these gaps being apparently widening at an alarming rate, a new era of technology transfer is said to be starting now, in an effort to remove obstacles to the transfer process, and to accelerate economic growth that is to bridge the disparity.

After two decades of development efforts, however, unemployment has emerged as the most critical problem of today in many developing countries. The disparity between the modern and the traditional sectors has proved of even greater magnitude than one had hoped that the developing societies would be able to tolerate. So, the question is, as Ul Haq puts it "if there is a dual economy, why not have a dual development strategy?". The modern sector may continue to struggle to reach advanced technological heights to narrow the gap vis-à-vis the developed countries. But for the traditional sector where the mass population abides, a more consciously inward-looking strategy may be pursued; there are indeed, an immense quantity of basic goods actually in demand for local consumption, and ways have to be found to affect more directly the indigenous life of the mass population where the development of technology does not have to be so fatally linked to international trade.

As mentioned in the previous section, the philosophy of alternative technology in the context of rural industrialisation breathes aloud behind such a dual development strategy. Thus, there is certainly great scope for technological policy consideration in attacking the problem of unemployment and income redistribution. However, many participants felt that the choice and adaptation of technology at the plant level might not be the only factor nor even the major factor in tackling the unemployment problem. Figueiredo, for example, appeared to prefer the even more simplistic statement that "employment growth should be absent from any design of policies related to selection and adaptation of technology". He meant to say that there were many other policy instruments designed more specifically to influence employment and income distribution: policies to promote the development of backward regions, policies to promote the export of manufactures, policies to promote the productivity of agriculture, etc. Technology policies are indeed not meant to be an alternative to those other development policies, and in reality none of them are to act in isolation. We all admit the obvious need for designing and effecting all these policies simultaneously and in harmony with the basic aspiration of the society, expressed in such a catch-all term as "development". But

the question remains: has "development" actually been effective
in combatting unemployment in many LDCs? And, as Sabato puts it,
there is an even more basic question that has long made us feel
uneasy: should be not have a better understanding of the relationship, be it called theoretical or practical, between technology
and economic policy?

Now, let us focus our attention on the industrial sector,
and the differential use of technology in small and large firms
within this sector - the phenomenon of industrial dualism is well
evidenced, and may thus be treatable in a less ideological fashion.
The Economic Growth Centre of Yale University has produced a
unique set of empirical studies referring to such countries as
the Republic of Korea, Pakistan, Taiwan, Mexico, Columbia, etc.
They demonstrate that the medium and small firms are in fact more
"efficient" in terms of the intensive use of scarce capital, and
that real industrial economies of scale are often exaggerated even
in industries in which continuous processes are dominant. Also,
small farmers and industrialists have no lower rates of saving and
capital accumulation than larger ones, so that the Galenson-
Leibenstein type of pessimism against labour-intensive technology
is not tenable without a substantial number of exceptions. In fact,
the Galenson-Leibenstein pessimism reflected only our first look
across the majority of the LDCs during the 1950s and 1960s when
primary and secondary import substitution was a more or less
typical pattern of development effort(1). It could be misleading
unless interpreted in its proper historical perspective.

Thus, Ranis draws our attention to the contemporary Korean
and Taiwanese cases where "export substitution" began to signal
the end of the import substitution phase already in 1959 and in
1963 respectively. In Taiwan the major policy changes, including
the devaluation and interest rate reform in 1959, resulted in a
quantum jump of labour-intensive industrial exports (textiles,
wood products and electronics) up to 70 per cent of total exports
by 1969, while the proportion of traditional rice and sugar shrank
from 78 per cent to less than 5 per cent of total export earnings
during the same period.

---

1) In Gustav Ranis' terminology "primary" import substitution
   means the import substitution in non-durable consumer goods,
   and "secondary" in durable consumer goods, capital and intermediate goods.

In the case of the Republic of Korea, the devaluation in 1964, and the doubling of interest rate in the following year, marked a shift towards the dramatic changes in output mix and technology that characterised the beginning of the export substitution phase. The export of labour-intensive electronics, textiles and footwear rose in 1968 to 80 per cent of total exports, the latter themselves growing at nearly 40 per cent annually. The rate of industrial labour absorption accelerated to 7 to 8 per cent annually in the 1960s in both countries; thus the share of employment in agriculture decreased from 56 per cent in 1953 to 40 per cent in 1968 in Taiwan, and from 68 per cent in 1955 to 51 per cent in 1968 in Korea. Domestic saving rates, as well as growth performances, rose palpably during the same period in both countries. Ranis takes this record as evidence that, with matured entrepreneurs and a competitive environment for them, a more endowment-sensitive choice and adaptation of technology can emerge, contributing simultaneously to both growth and employment objectives[1].

The above case histories suggest that an LDC at the import substitution phase, busy responding to the initial shortage of domestic entrepreneurship and overhead capital, will normally find only a limited scope for choice in technology borrowing, while there may exist substantial scope for technological assimilation, particularly indigenous innovation in a labour-using and capital-saving direction. This latter potential tends to remain under-exploited for some time, however, until domestic entrepreneurial capacity (and certain essential infrastructures) matures enough to stand the hardships of competitive business that would ensue were the earlier capital-cheap, protectionist policies to be eliminated. In terms of policy implications, it is logically clear that the policies which make capital artificially cheap and labour artificially expensive have the effect of inhibiting the search for endowment-sensitive technology and output mix. More realistic relative-prices are perhaps a necessary, if not sufficient, condition for inducing a more appropriate use of technology. Thus, an LDC, if it is to follow the lessons given by the Korean and Taiwanese experience, will have to face up sooner or later to a politically difficult decision towards import liberalisation and

1) G. Ranis, "Some Observations on the Economic Framework for Optimum LDC Utilisation of Technology", the Economic Growth Centre Discussion Paper No. 152, Yale University. This paper was presented also at the 23rd May Seminar on Economics and Technology at Washington, D.C., organised by the US AID.

curtailment of fiscal incentives, if only gradually.

There are a number of LDCs in Africa, which have yet to complete the primary import substitution phase. Would there be any lessons for them to learn from those "deviant" cases if they wished to evoke the beginning of an export substitution phase more quickly than the Ranis "stage theory" could predict?(1) Admittedly, these case histories are not meant to provide answers to these questions. But they offer a perspective against which other countries could appraise their current development strategy and probe new policies to cope with their own situation. How gradual should the gradual liberalisation be? When, and how, can a country judge itself to be ready for such policy shifts?

The irony of fate, as far as those deviant cases are concerned (and one could further add to them the historical case of Japan after the turn of the century, the Mexican Border Programme, etc.), is that the primary export substitution began apparently in less privileged segments of the industrial economy, whose efficiency and comparative advantage were accounted for to a considerable extent by the discipline of hard-working, low-waged industrial work forces, and the ever-present threat of the "reserve army" outside that helped maintain it. Would it be fair to say that the endowment sensitive technical innovations in these segments of the economy are to be induced by a policy of negligence that keeps them exposed to the "realistic" factor prices (costly capital and cheap labour?) In all these cases, there continued to co-exist a more privileged sector where capital-intensive technology choices remained dominant. The activities in the latter "privileged" sector appear to involve a more or less strong element of infrastructural investment; be it called the option for "effets d'entraînement" or the "psychological barrier" vis-à-vis the technology gap facing these countries. Today, many LDCs recognise the need for a new technology policy for at least part of the public sector as well. Thus, ILO is about to complete a manual for endowment-sensitive techniques of road construction(2). The UN Advisory Committee for Application of Science and Technology has decided to have its Working Group on

---

1) Frances Stewart's comment on this subject is: "Ranis examples are all special cases - small countries, with skilled and educated (and Chinese) populations, close to rapidly growing markets. Thus the results may not be generalisable.

2) See Scope, Approach and Content of Research-Oriented Activities of the World Employment Programme, International Labour Office, Geneva, 1972.

Appropriate Technology examine in depth the problem of public (especially rural) housing(1). A growing interest is emerging in the policies and techniques of technology management of local industries in Mainland China. Alongside these inward-looking new policy orientations with the public sector, however, if a country expects to find some leading agents for export substitution in the private sector, particularly small and medium size entrepreneurs, then a "fair game" should be played that would match the very significance of their role. But how fair is fair?

As Ranis points out, fiscal incentives, such as the case of India's Khadi, may be destined to fail. Will the Appropriate Technology Cell, and other "direct actions" to induce adaptive progress, have a better chance? Will it be a necessary condition to keep in force a substantial degree of competition (even to the extent that small businesses themselves often consider it as "excessive"), in order to let the generally short-sighted, profit-greedy small businesses achieve as a whole, the kind of objective that is visible only from the standpoint of the national economy? Adaptative innovations that live up to the pressure of domestic competition would leave behind them dropouts and frictional unemployment, and some social problems associated with those defeated. "How fair is the fair game?" is by no means a new question. This is the question that has long hovered over those concerned with small industries, in both advanced and developing economies.

As Frances Stewart has pointed out, however, although competition was an important aspect of many of the countries considered, another important factor was the subcontracting from the protected sector. This could not occur without a protected sector. It does seem from these cases that the process of sub-contracting between the sectors is important and needs more study. The Chinese (Mainland) case provides an alternative model (without, it appears, the profit maximisation and competitive element), as mentioned earlier, but disregarded here.

One important issue from the aggregate economic point of view is to consider how far the export substituting activities relate to the import substituting and public activities. In the Ranis schema, the former are causally and temporally subsequent to the latter, so that one can think of "phases". In the first, import substituting, phase previously non-existent entrepreneurial skills

---

1) See UNACAST, Record of the Seventeenth Session, 23rd October - 1st November, 1972, Chapter II, Section 3.

are developed while a minimum physical and human environment is put in place for the subsequent development of internationally competitive industries. There are sceptics, however, who wonder how far the second phase activities really are dependent on the first. Indeed, it is frequently argued that, on the contrary, some import substituting/infrastructure building strategies actually pursued in the 1950s and 1960s did lasting damage to the potential internationally competitive activities. It is difficult to trace the benefit that export industries such as electronics, textiles, processed food or handicrafts in India, Pakistan or Turkey, have derived from the establishment in those countries of steel mills, nuclear power stations, heavy mechanical, heavy electrical and machine tool industries. It is equally difficult to trace the benefits of the massive investments in human resource developments (technical universities and institutes, government laboratories) in these countries. These investments have, almost inevitably, a long gestation period, and their relations with the "export-substituting" endowment-sensitive activities may be too indirect to be made tractable from the policy standpoint. However, if we cannot trace the connections it is difficult to see how the import substituting/infrastructure building activities are causally and temporally prior. To the extent that one is sceptical of this causal and temporal priority, the Ranis schema collapses. Perhaps the export-substituting/endowment-sensitive activities should proceed simultaneously with the import-substituting/infrastructure-building activities.

One can still retain the idea of "duality" in overall economic (and technology) policies. Fiscal and monetary policies combine with administrative devices in many LDCs to give massive effective protection and subsidies to selected import-substituting/infra-structure-building activities, on the assumption that this support will pay off in the long term. This part of a "dualist strategy" is relatively straightforward. (However, it has its sceptics - who doubt whether the amount of support actually given is necessary or whether the benefits justify it or, still worse, whether it is not generally given in practice for bad political reasons.) The difficult problem is to relate such a strategy to the strategy for other sectors of the economy. Clearly, with some qualifications about the fungibility of external resources, support for the favoured sectors represents a resource transfer from other sectors. And, from a public investment planning point of view, investment is promoted in the favoured sectors at the expense of some less

favoured sectors: here the qualification is partly about the
fungibility of domestic investment funds. How important these
fungibility constraints are in practice seems a very difficult
issue to resolve in most LDCs.

In the practice of development planning, however, the trade-
off between the "dual" sectors does not generally seem an immediate
issue. Partly this is because the costs of supporting the favoured
sectors are diffused through the economy in higher prices, higher
taxes, physical scarcities and administrative inefficiencies. The
endowment-sensitive activities may be affected directly through
restrained domestic (or international) demand for their products,
through higher bought with input costs or through greater administrative inefficiency. This type of relations between sectors in a
"dualist" economy is not adequately researched and discussion of
it tends more than usually to reflect inadequately articulated
value judgments (about the role of the public sector, national
independence, "modernisation", the sort of products that should
be produced). However, it seems that there has been a tendency in
practice to ignore these general effects, on traditional endowment-
sensitive activities, of promotion of the modern sector.

Now, questions of macro-economic strategy apart, let us turn
our attention for a while to the sources and channels of technological assimilation of small industries. The process of technology
transfer is generally more complicated in the case of the small and
medium sized firms which have originated in localised traditional
markets. To the extent that these firms have started with an element of special technology of local origin, the pattern of their
subsequent technological evolution contrasts with that of the
larger firms starting with modern imported technology. Small firms
showed a tendency to grow around a number of regional poles in the
history of many advanced countries. In Japan, for example, nearly
300 regional poles (called "Sanchi") were discernible, each known
for its special traditional know-how; some in metal tableware,
some in chinaware, some in spinning, and many in food processing.
Little is yet documented about the pattern of diffusion of new
technology within and across these poles. On the whole, however,
it seems that the diffusion process has not only been more complicated, but much slower than in the case of large-scale oligopolists.

Operating in a relatively unprivileged sector of the economy
(with limited access to capital and technical skill), unimaginative
entrepreneurs plead for cheaper money rather than to respond to
the modernisation campaign. Operating with limited modules of

production technology, imaginative innovations will occur more frequently in small tools and apparatus, labour management and marketing techniques, than in machine designs and process engineering. But much of the innovations achieved in the form of managerial and operating skills may be lost with business discontinuities. Large firms which seek subcontractors for jobs of limited scope may do so simply to save incremental capital costs for their capacity expansion; but this process as a whole may serve the purpose of isolating from new technology those elements or modules which are more "permeable" to small entrepreneurs while forcing these entrepreneurs to work out the most efficient uses of old modules in combination with the new elements. Those who probe a more technology-conscious approach to small industry policies would certainly welcome an in-depth empirical study in this matter.

Apparently, there is great scope for transfer of technology from the small-industrial firms in advanced countries to those in developing countries. Such transfer may take place through various types of contract, such as commercial know-how contracts, subcontracting, joint ventures, arrangements through public promotion and extension services, etc. According to the enquiry recently concluded by the Federal Ministry for Economic Cooperation of Germany (1), there exist a sizable number of firms of small to medium size interested in opportunities for cooperation with firms in developing countries. Most of these firms are in the branches of industry which are statistically characterised by high wage bills relative to value added, and workers "without specialised training" in the production process. Stangen points out that they are not fully aware of the international scene and mostly lacking in experience in finding their foreign partners; but they consider the high wages in Germany as an important motive for their interest in transfer of technology – in contrast to those firms which have already got involved in joint ventures with developing countries (for the latter, to open up new markets is cited as a major motive and the idea of re-exporting has been practically absent in their motivation as yet). Among those firms which have so far had some experience in technical cooperation with developing countries about one-third transferred mainly modern techniques of production, and one-third mainly simple techniques or techniques no longer practised in Germany. In both cases, "size of market" is, as usual, a dominant factor underlying the choice.

---

1) Based on Fritz Stangen's personal report.

In the case of small firms, particularly those without experience or ability to find overseas partners for themselves, public promotion measures will indeed play an important role. It is still questionable, however, how far the situations resulting from such transfer will be different from those connected with multinational corporations.

When the transfer takes the form of profit-seeking direct foreign investment by small entrepreneurs, there will be a host of questions to be cleared about the real motivation of individual cases. Realising that small entrepreneurs tend to have relatively short time horizons in their economic calculations, some of these questions might prove even less tractable than in the case of large multinational corporations. In the case of technical co-operation without capital participation, to utilise small industry talents in isolation from the particular business environment in which they have lived would generally be a difficult task. Exportable talents, if any, may already have entered a new profession of industrial consultancy (and in many instances such people might be better qualified as management consultants than as engineering consultants). If emphasis is on particular production techniques and equipment used in small industries, the information-service type of cooperation may be more readily practicable as a modality of official aid in this field. But information can only flow effectively when there are sufficient entrepreneurships and industrial infrastructures for assimilation and adaptation at the receiving end. In regard to adaptive technological research, a conceivable aid project may consist in mobilising the research facilities of various specialised laboratories and engineering institutes (within a given donor country) through some special network activated by a small central unit - the idea being currently examined quite seriously in certain OECD Member countries (e.g. the scientific cooperation programme of the Federal Ministry for Economic Cooperation of Germany; the "Institute for Transfer of Industrial Technology" project of the Ministry of International Trade and Industry of Japan). But such an approach, too, will need the support of a broader imaginative programme that looks into the risk-taking capacity of LDC industrialists for commercial application of particular technology.

Out of these reflections, one would start wondering "why small firms?" Indeed, in many respects, the distinction between small and large firms may prove quite immaterial. Still more so when one deals with the transfer of technology through foreign investment.

A key question would be: what is that special thing that one looks for in the transfer of technology to LDCs directly originating from small firms in advanced countries? The relatively labour-intensive techniques of production being used, or once used by these firms constitute an important factor indeed. But only part of this factor would be susceptible to the "engineering handbook" type of treatment. Even large multinational corporations could play an equally important role in the transfer of that kind of knowledge. What is then the remaining part? Perhaps much of it is attributable to the resilient entrepreneurship and the tactical ingenuity in capital-saving technical development which have survived domestic and international competition in the relatively unprivileged corners of the economy.

Chapter III

MULTINATIONAL CORPORATIONS : THE INFANCY OF EMPIRICAL RESEARCH

Those who acclaim the multinational corporation (MNC) as an agent of development, and those who wish to condemn it as a weapon of exploitation would both agree that it has now become an extremely powerful agent of technology transfer. The consolidation of major producers' positions from material supplies production technologies to marketing and management seems to have so easily moved across national frontiers. Thus rather hastily, an eminent U.S. economist predicted that "the nation state is just about through as an economic unit."(1) Exciting as it was, the prediction, as well as the heated controversy which immediately followed it, entailed an element of "misdemeanor" of arguing by exaggeration, and the excitement itself revealed perhaps a symptom of the infancy of empirical research in this domain.

The MNCs have exhibited the dynamics of the mature industrial economies which seek continual innovation in methods of stimulating

---

1) C.P. Kindleberger, <u>American Business Abroad : Six Lectures on Direct Investment</u>, New Haven and London, 1969, p. 207.

consumers' demand with new products, new designs, and new marketing arrangements. However, innovation of this kind is not entirely in line with real LDC needs. In the terminology of IREP Grenoble (Judet and Palloix)(1), the internationalisation via multinational firms brings out a partial, and often non-rooted "extraversion" of the LDC economy, which frustrates the more natural, "intra-verted" industrialisation efforts so much needed. The extraversion results in a distortion of both consumers' demand and technological choices, since the impact of the MNC will generally be strongest in those sectors where foreign know-how can be readily applied, and weakest in sectors like tropical agriculture, handicrafts, small industries, the use of local by-products, etc. It creates and deepens the dualism, by playing havoc with the local factor price structure, and minimising interactions with the unskilled, unreliable and undisciplined local labour behing its seemingly generous, philanthropic contributions.

Indeed, there are a number of possible sources of conflict between the multinational corporation and the host country that appear easily visible on an a priori ground. The obvious sources are, as Paul Streeten once pointed out(2),

   i)   the fact that the multinational is 'private', with the urge to make profits;

  ii)   that it is 'large and oligopolistic', with overwhelmingly strong bargaining power;

iii)   that it is 'foreign' in terms of its locus of ownership and control; and

 iv)   that it is 'foreign' again in terms of the origin of its technology, with its products, know-how, use of materials, management practices all pre-adapted to foreign conditions.

The fact that these a priori sources of conflict can account for the pessimistic attitudes of many does not immediately imply that the balance of advantage should always be negative in practice. Of course, it is not an easy notion to grasp. Even the "nation state" has different interest groups within it that align themselves differently with foreign-owned firms. If it is possible for the

---

1) Background Paper No. 33.

2) Paul Streeten, "Costs and Benefits of Multinational Enterprises in Less Developed Countries", in John H. Dunning, etc., The Multinational Enterprise, London, George Allen and Unwin, 1971, p. 251.

host country to control the MNC so as to curtail its damaging effects and to reap its beneficial effects, does its government have the necessary political power to do so? If it has both the power and the will, then does it have the necessary expertise to do so? In the absence of an unequivocal answer to these basic questions in many LDCs, the MNC problems would appear certainly more acute than when envisaged among developed countries.

A degree of divergence appeared to exist among the participants in the November Study Group with respect to their attitudes to the question of multinational corporations. Although the exposition offered by Judet and Palloix on their "working hypotheses" concerning MNC behaviour sounded like that of a radical denunciator, it did not particularly surprise the Group; nor perhaps, did the Group as a whole find it very illuminating. Rather than choosing between the theme of the "Schumpeterian protagonists" and that of the "nationalist antagonists", many participants seemed to be interested in finding areas between the two susceptible to empirical research. For example, for those concerned with the question of tax concessions, a question of empirical significance would be: to what extent would MNCs ask for protection against imports in order for them to produce in an LDC for the domestic market.

Livelier discussion arose in fact around the question whether multinational firms were less likely than domestic firms to adapt their technology to local conditions. Multinational firms, with their greater technological competence and experience, could be an efficient agent for satisfying the LDC need for adaptive innovations, if they were given a proper incentive to do so. They might be generally less preoccupied with employing the latest technology, on account of their greater market power. These considerations would indeed be amenable to empirically researchable hypotheses. In this context, an interesting study by Howard Pack on Kenyan industries was recalled(1). Some of the plants operated by multinational corporations in Kenya, particularly those corporations having substantial experience with production in LDCs, adopt capital-saving methods to optimise the use of low-cost labour, and are even on the lookout for inexpensive second-hand equipment, whereas local entrepreneurs, whose background is commercial rather than technical, often overlook such opportunities.

---

1) Howard Pack, "The Use of Labour Intensive Techniques in Kenyan Industry", in Technology and Economics in International Development, Agency for International Development, Washington, D.C., May 1972.

Another case in point is the Dutch electronics firm, Philips, which has a special laboratory in the Netherlands to adapt technology to local production circumstances in specific LDCs. This firm has adopted, for its plants located in certain LDCs, process designs for core production that are considered already obsolete in Europe but perfectly economically viable under the factor price relations in particular LDCs. Some participants (e.g. Gerard Boon) appeared very much impressed by the aptitude of MNC policy-makers to take into account differences in factor prices and cost minimisation criteria in their planning of production location. Boon also drew attention to some of the MNCs in the electronics and automotive industries operating in Mexico: the types of technology and the adaptations introduced by these corporations were indicative of their sensitivity to differences in lot size and production volume as well as factor prices.

The National Academy of Sciences and the National Academy of Engineering of the U.S. are undertaking an extensive study concerning MNC interest and involvement in LDC technological development. The interim report by Daniel Margolies indicates that this study draws on a group of panels concerned with various industrial sectors such as electronics, pharmaceuticals, food processing, automotive, chemicals, construction equipment, etc. It is already possible to cite a number of examples of adaptive engineering in product design and development by U.S. based MNCs: the Argentine and the Brazilian plants of the National Cash Register Company; clinical testing and product development programmes of multinationals in the pharmaceutical industry; the multipurpose transport vehicle developed by Ford and General Motors; the DNT tractor of Ford, the low-cost, rugged communications system developed by a subsidiary of Northrop; etc. These feature, however, adaptive innovation efforts on a regional or collective basis, rather than the results of research geared to unique requirements within specific individual developing countries.

On an individual country basis, MNCs have made more impressive contributions

i) by providing in-house training programmes for their employees and
ii) by philanthropic support to local foundations devoted to advancement of local scientific education and research.

The survey of the Council of Americas, recently completed, gave a long list of examples of such contributions. There are also evidences that these training and educational programmes are not particularly tied to the interest of the particular donor corporations, but that a substantial proportion of those trained by a MNC are moving out to take employment with other firms and industries. Thus, Margolies concludes that "there is no question that the multinational corporations have exerted a powerful influence within the countries where they operate for upgrading the quality of managerial and technical performance."[1] However, mainly due to the limited size of market, research and development by the U.S. based multinational corporations solely or primarily directed to an individual LDC is still much less impressive. Margolies cites several examples such as: the banana and palm oil research laboratory of the United Fruit Company in Honduras, the rubber plantation laboratory of the Firestone Rubber Company in Liberia, the research staff built up by an Argentine affiliate of the General Tyre and Rubber Company, the Golden Macaroni project of the General Food Corporation for its Brazilian affiliate, the Corn Products programme of the CPC International in Colombia and Brazil, etc. Not all these research programmes were carried out within the host LDCs, but the number of examples will increase considerably if we include adaptive research and innovation conducted in the U.S. and other advanced countries' own laboratories specifically directed towards the interest of the developing world in general.

Referring to the results of these recent surveys, Schweitzer noted that these cheerful evidences might not be taken at their face value since they were not intended to describe the representative performances of the U.S. multinational firms; cheerful cases are still relatively few in number and rather isolated in their pattern of occurrence, and would perhaps be easily overwhelmed by a mass of more dismal evidence, should one make an equally methodical attempt to look into the latter. However, what interests us at this moment is not whether the defense should win the case, but rather in finding out in further detail what special factors and actors did actually account for those cases in which MNCs had relatively better performances in relation to the LDC interest. The fact that successful product adaptations by MNCs have taken place more frequently on a regional or collective basis than to cope with the limited market of an individual LDC, suggests that increased cooperation between LDCs themselves would be necessary

1) "Multinational Corporations and Adaptive Research for Developing Countries", in Appropriate Technologies for International Development : Preliminary Survey of Research Activities, US AID, Washington, D.C. September, 1972.

to secure a market large enough for serious industrial research and innovation as well as for fair bargaining with multinational corporations.

On the part of MNCs themselves, there is yet little indication of the possibility of enforcing any world-wide code of business conduct for the transfer of technology. It is doubtful if the governments of advanced countries are themselves at present in a position to permit effective enforcement of such a code on their big businesses. It is also not at all clear what provisions such a code might have in practice, nor how effective it could be: this would depend upon its interaction with other factors in the bargaining process in particular transfer situations. But there seems to exist wide support for the view that both the governments and the firms of developed countries have become increasingly aware of the basic needs of their poorer partners. With the creation of a new Inter-governmental Group on the Transfer of Technology, complaints on restrictive business practices will be registered more loudly and more publicly. Even if this will not immediately lead to an international code of conduct and a regulatory machinery for it, it is quite likely that the MNCs will become an object of study with growing intensity.

Today, it is perhaps the lack of information about the operations of multinational corporations, and not the ideological discrepancy, that inhibits a thorough assessment of their true role. Inflated transfer prices through intracorporate sales, location of profits, etc., impose a great deal of statistical difficulty. The information problems are particularly acute where there are only a few major international competitors left in an industry. Research to secure more facts on benefits and costs of specific arrangements between MNCs and their host countries should receive high priority among the functions to be performed by way of international action at this stage.

Chapter IV

PRICE OF TECHNOLOGY : PROBLEM IDENTIFICATION

"Technology is a product which is bought and sold" (Sabato). Most participants did not find this slogan surprising, but one

could not claim that there was great clarity in it. What it intends
to say may have been simply that the technology transfer and adaptation process needs to be demythologised and that one should think
of foreign technology in a particular situation as a range of products which may or may not be bought at prices that one may or may
not be able to influence.

Pursuing that product analogy, participants overwhelmingly
agreed that the technology market is an imperfect one, with important oligopolistic practices. (There may be situations, too, where
the market exhibits monopsonist/oligopsonist practices, but this
is seldom discussed in relation to the LDC situation in general.)
The statement that the market is imperfect may not by itself be
much of an enlightenment. There are only one or two important
generalisations one can draw about imperfect markets: viz:

a)   that price exceeds marginal cost; and
b)   that with **oligopoly** (as against imperfect competition)
     there is an indeterminacy about price, which is subject
     to bargaining strategy and games theory.

These both seem relevant to technology markets.

The UNCTAD Secretariat, unfortunately not represented at the
Study Group, made a study of the costs of technology transfer to
developing countries for the April 1972 UNCTAD III Conference(1).
This study identifies six types of cost incurred by the receiving
country:

i)   for the right to use patents, licences, know-how and
      trade marks;

ii)   for technical knowledge and know-how at the pre-investment
      and operational stages;

iii) for price increases in intra-company sales;

iv)   for profits capitalised in the acquisition of shares
      in the "receiving" company;

v)   for some part of the profit of fully foreign owned sub-
      sidiaries which have no special provisions to pay for
      technology transfers from the price;

vi)   for overpricing of capital goods and equipment.

---

1)   "Technology transfer", report by the UNCTAD Secretariat,
     TD/106, 10th November, 1972.

Since most of the available information is, first, fragmentary and, second, refers only to (i) and (ii) above, the UNCTAD estimates may be considered as an understatement of the total cost of technology transfer. For thirteen countries (including Spain and Turkey), the identifiable foreign exchange payments corresponding to the first two items had reached $643 million annually by the end of the 1960s, representing 4.5 per cent of their countries' total export earnings and 0.36 per cent of their GDP. A crude adjustment for the more obvious omissions would suggest that the real figures for the thirteen countries was around $960 million. Making an even cruder adjustment to cover (i) other LDCs and (ii) the items generally not covered, the UNCTAD paper puts total LDC technology transfer payments in 1968 (excluding Spain and Turkey) at some $1.5 billion(1). Should it be plausible to expect a 20 per cent per annum growth in such technology transfer payments, then, on the DD II strategy assumption of a 7 per cent annual average growth in export earnings, the share of technology transfer payments in total exports might rise from 5 per cent at the end of the 1960s to some 15 per cent at the end of the 1970s.

The UNCTAD Secretariat contention that their estimates understate the real cost may not be argued _a priori_. The net "cost" incurred under points (iii) to (vi) above could be negative in some situations. Not all cases of technology transfer to LDCs have been profitable for the technology supplying country. (There is some evidence of a range of situations in which the technology supplying companies are operating at the unstable end of the oligopolistic market, being prepared to sell below cost to sustain a market). It is questionable, however, whether this instability problem is actually so important vis-à-vis the LDC market as often emphasised by multinational corporate strategists.   If the net additional (or hidden) cost is likely to be higher under normal circumstances, then, there is still an important question, how high is high? Relative to which alternatives?

Much of the discussion about the cost of technology transfer has assumed implicitly that one can forget about the use made of the technology when assessing the cost of the transfer. Thoumi's paper and intervention at the Study Group offered a relatively extreme version of this view. For him, the cost of technology is

---

1)   F. Thoumi, "The International Market of Technology, Direct Foreign Investment, Market Structures and Policies for Less Developed Countries", (Background Paper No. 6).

something that can be determined almost exclusively on the basis
of research and development costs involved in it; "the amount of
technology possessed by a firm or person can be increased at a
very low marginal cost, that is, it can enjoy the external economies generated by the firm or person that created the technology"(1).

Thoumi argues that there could not be a competitive market in
technology since the amount of technology that could be competitively produced would be negligible, and pricing technology at
marginal costs would seldom cover total costs. In these circumstances, in order to maximise welfare, the government should subsidise the production of technology while imposing marginal pricing
for its transfer. At the same time, he argues that LDC governments
should establish national (or multinational) technological centres
which would acquire technology (at whatever price they could get
it) and "make it available to the users at marginal costs". Some
other participants (Gonod, Judet) who advocated LDC national (or
international) technology centres probably believed, at least
partly, in the Thoumi thesis about the market characteristics of
technology. However, one could stop short of the assertion that
marginal costs are almost negligible. Others have argued that LDCs
are obliged to make "repetitive" imports of the same technology
(thus paying several times) because of restrictions placed on the
use of a particular technology by the patent holder or process
licensor. The establishment of national technology centres may well
strengthen the bargaining position of LDC buyers. The market might
be made much more competitive simply by much better information
and much more experience among those responsible for acquiring
technology.

While technology may be a product or a range of products,
several participants were concerned to stress the extent to which
the products are wrapped up into packages in the sellers' market.
At its worst, the package wraps up into one single deal, the process,
its design and engineering, the provision of equipment and know-how,
a supply of raw materials and intermediates, and the provision of
markets; the package may also be wrapped up institutionally by the
links between process licensor (usually a major international
producer of the product), engineering firm and the equipment
supplier. "Turn-key" contracts may thus have many ways of raising
the price of technology transfer to the recipient country.

---

1) F. Thoumi, "The International Market of Technology, Direct
   Foreign Investment, Market Structures and Policies for Less
   Developed Countries", (Background Paper No. 6).

Today, few disfavour the theme of "unpacking technology" as far as possible, if only because this is a sign of the buyer's maturity. It does not, however, follow that buying a package always inflates the total cost of the items included, or that some of the items are redundant. Still less does it follow that it is necessarily wrong to pay a higher aggregate price for a package than for its identifiable elements. It is not likely that the results from use of a package will be the same as if its elements were bought separately (and used together with those developed locally). Clearly the desirability of different alternatives will vary from situation to situation. Should a country be lacking in the technological and industrial capabilities needed to buy any-thing other than a comprehensive turn-key contract for the execu-tion of a given development programme, the question it should first resolve will be whether or not to execute such a programme at all.

Thus, a wider doubt concerns the extent to which it is useful to think of the price of technology in isolation from the whole context of its use. The economic evaluation of technological alter-natives would require cost and benefit calculations about the use to which the alternatives are to be put. And if one gets serious about such cost/benefit calculations for a project or an operation, the particular use may itself be subject to consideration against its alternatives. The UNCTAD Secretariat estimates of the foreign exchange cost of technology transfer are highly meaningful in pointing out that some relatively large sums are involved, perhaps threatening the LDC debt service ratios or suggesting changes in investment priorities. The estimates thus serve the purpose of increasing "cost consciousness" in transfer of technology. Better bargaining would indeed help to the extent that many LDCs lack the necessary administrative talent. But the price question becomes relevant only at one, perhaps concluding, stage of technology transfer contracts.

In this connection, one may consider the important OAS Pilot Project, introduced by Gonod, which envisages a broader range of functions to be fulfilled for successful transfer of technology:

i) to identify the participating enterprises and institutions and the specific projects considered for technology transfer;

ii) to transmit the existing (explicit) technological demands of the participating enterprises and institutions between a National and the Regional (multinational) Focal Points, together with possible solutions;

iii) to detect potential (implicit) technological requirements
of the participating enterprises;

iv) to provide technological information and technical
assistance to the national firms and to make the evaluation of alternative technologies taking into account
local social and market costs;

v) to improve the negotiation capability of the enterprises
in the acquisition of technology and assist them in the
purchase of technology. As part of this task, assistance
should be provided to "open the package" of technology
and to find different sources for appropriate technol-
ogies(1).

Thus, the issues about the appropriate choice of technology,
as they closely overlap with those about the transfer of technology,
stress the important pre-conditions for meaningful negotiation:
i.e. knowledge and assessment of the alternatives available for
analysis and policy. Also the interface mechanism between government, industrialists, and various professional research and intelligence agencies in both the public and the private sectors, will
be an important object of the study, as emphasised in the OAS
experiment.

However, reverting to the question of "hidden" price of technology transfer, there is obviously need for the excavation of
relevant micro-data in order to size up the conditions and parameters influencing the magnitude and variability of the various
indirect costs. At the time when a transfer contract is being concluded, possibly identifiable indirect charges will be related to
the procurement terms for raw and intermediate materials, equipment
and other capital goods. The terms of profit expatriation in the
case of foreign-owned subsidiaries may include an element of charges
on technology proper that one could isolate from the cost of
"capital" as such under certain assumptions. But isolation of the
"cost of technology" from the way in which benefits are actually
shared in the subsequent operating phase would frequently require
some heroic (sometimes even ideological) assumptions. The transfer

----

1) Note d'Information sur l'Organisation et l'Etat de Realisation
de Projet Pilote de Transfert de Technologie de l'Organisation
des Etats Americains. (Background Paper No.8).

of technology solely based on licence agreements (and with some explicit technical assistance agreements) might offer a theoretical benchmark against which other forms of contract involving capital participation might be examined. But this would not immediately open up scope for aggregative statistical analysis. For example, in Japan around 1960, the sales of products based on imported technologies constituted a very high proportion of the total sales of technology-intensive industries such as chemicals, electronics and machinery, while technology imports were predominantly through licence and know-how contracts without foreign capital participation. And the prices being paid for imported technology, relative to the total sales of industrial exports, remained almost constant (around 0.2 per cent). But while this kind of statistics would be meaningful as an indicator of the overall national capability of technological assimilation and adaptation, it would be only of the remotest relevance to the pricing of a particular imported technology.

As in the case of most issues related to multinational corporations in developing countries, a practical research methodology is probably desirable in securing and organising relevant empirical indepth information for a clearer problem definition on the price aspect of technology transfer. The UNCTAD Secretariat appear likely to conduct (or sponsor) further research involving individual country case studies. However, the current UNCTAD approach raises methodological and empirical problems of the types discussed above (e.g. some have argued that it tends to obscure possible links between costs and use of technology in different situations). The Development Centre is considering a research project in this area which initially would try to consider the practical methodological problems in the context of detailed country contract data, perhaps involving Argentina and Algeria.

Chapter V

CHOICE AND DIFFUSION OF TECHNOLOGY :
QUESTIONS BEYOND THE FACTOR PRICE DISTORTION

One often suspects there is something autonomous about technological innovations; at least some technical changes appear to be stimulated by autonomous discoveries in pure science, and this is particularly the case with the so-called science-based industries. Such a versatile inventor as Thomas Edison is said to have had no more imaginative economic forecast about the use of his phonograph than the possibility for old men to record their wishes on their death beds. Aeronautical technology is often cited as an example of the concept of a technological "leading" sector. One should not neglect, however, the fact that the technological multiplier effects of this sector have been particularly impressive in their military applications where cost constraints play a less important role than in the case of civil aviation, automobiles, etc.(1) While neo-classical economics has certainly tended to make technical change exogeneous, one would recall that Adam Smith's specialisation took the form of technical change and was a response to (and cause of) changing economic variables. For Marx, and for Schumpeter, technology was not a completely exogeneous variable. Inventors may not respond to economic incentives, but Schmookler has shown that patented inventions do respond. The commercial development and application of new ideas clearly is responsive to economic factors.

Perhaps little remains debatable about the importance of factor prices in the choice of technology as long as one remains within the framework of the generalised theory of the firm under conditions of perfect competition. In dealing with the textile industry where LDCs can have choices from a wide range of known technological alternatives of various vintages, de Bandt argued that factor price distortions should be a central issue in the discussion of LDC technology policy(2). Many other participants noted, however, that the issue would not be treatable meaningfully unless one settled the question of differential strategies in the public and the private sectors of the economy.

De Bandt argued that foreign aid on soft financial terms was a major source of underpricing of capital in LDCs. Some other participants wondered whether foreign aid is ever a major source of underpricing. It is frequently argued that tied aid (and some nominally untied aid) leads to massive over-pricing of capital goods in relation to their international prices. (De Bandt argues that this actually aggravates the problem, with the result that

_____

1) See, e.g. Jean Parent, Background Paper No. 14.
2) Background Paper No. 4.

capital intensivy may actually be higher in LDCs than DCs: see his note in Part **Two**). Schweitzer suggested that only a comparatively small proportion of such official aid was used to support directly sectors strongly motivated by financial profitability (such as large-scale private industrial sectors). /He might have added that the final recipient of the aid frequently does not receive the concessional financial terms because the finance passes through one or more intermediary (e.g. the central government or a public investment bank)._/ However, technology choices could be distorted indirectly through capital underpricing in utilities or other infrastructure. Few participants - de Bandt was the principal exception - seemed to favour the suggestion that the price of labour should be subsidised to correct the capital/labour price distortion. Apart from not knowing what the shadow wage rate should be, most participants were impressed by the administrative (even political) difficulty of subsidising unskilled labour wages. Stewart, moreover, argued that there was a risk of creating a still worse factor price distortion if unskilled labour costs were sub-sidised in the large-scale modern industrial sector but not in the traditional small-scale sector.

Even though the theory of the firm makes it clear how an "economic man" should behave, it is much less clear how business-men actually do behave. Stepanek suggested, for example, that the type of technology used in LDC sugar refineries depended very much on who owned the production and marketing: if it was a large "capitalist" producer, the product would probably be relatively highly refined white sugar and the scale of production relatively large. It is frequently said that the subsidiaries of foreign firms operating in LDCs are generally insensitive to local factor prices in determining the technology they use. If the residual variation unexplained by the behavioural principle of the economic man should be very large, then there will be little scope for amending the actual pattern of technological choice by a corrective policy on factor prices. While the November meeting was not presented with any empirical evidence to support the debate, an interesting case study of L.T. Wells, Jr. was later brought to our attention[1].

---

1) L.T. Wells,Jr., "Economic Man and Engineering Man : Choice of Technology in a Low Wage Country", in Economic Development Report, Harvard Development Advisory Service, Cambridge, Mass., Autumn 1972.

The study of Wells, Jr., deals with a sample of 50 industrial plants in Indonesia, covering such industries as cigarettes, soft drink bottling, plastic sandals, bicycle and tyres, woven bags, and flashlight batteries. It attempts to question the rationale for the different technologies co-existing in the country: e.g. in the cigarette manufacture, three classes of technology are operating side by side - the capital intensive class using on the average three workers per million cigarettes, the labour intensive class for which the estimate averages at 40, and the intermediate class employing six workers per million cigarettes. The actual factor price market is such an imperfect one that the differential wage rates applicable to foreign, domestic state-owned, and domestic private firms are 0.75, 0.55 and 0.30 US $/day, respectively in the case of unskilled workers; 1.22, 1.02 and 0.85 US $/day in the case of skilled workers. Subsidised capital at 12 per cent annual interest is accessible to those firms which have chosen relatively sophisticated technology, while the market rates of 24 to 36 per cent are applicable to most other domestic competitors. However, according to his estimates the incremental investment needed to shift from hand bottling of soft drink to semi-automatic bottling, for example, was of the order of $833 per worker saved, or approximately $380 in terms of annual capital and maintenance cost (at 36 per cent interest rate and 10 per cent maintenance or depreciation per year) - a figure considerably above the wage rate in Indonesia. The calculations made for critical processes in the various industries indicate further that the shift from the "intermediate" to the "capital-intensive" class of technology would require an incremental investment of $6,986 on the average ($21,500 for the highest) per worker saved. Even if an industrialist could raise capital abroad at 8 per cent interest rate, the corresponding annual cost of such investment (including 10 per cent depreciation per annum) would be $1,260 ($3,850 for the highest) per worker to be saved. Even with a high allowance for social costs, it is unlikely that the real cost of a worker could approach this figure in Indonesia.

Wells makes a careful check of other economic factors that are a priori relevant for the choice of technology: i.e.

a) the cost of developing more labour-intensive techniques;
b) the quality of product; and
c) the raw material saving possibility with automated process technology.

These factors were found generally much less important than, for example, the monopolistic advantage of the use of international trade names which overshadows the price advantage of intermediate and labour-intensive technology in competition. Still more important proves to be the built-in bias of managers and engineers in favour of capital-intensive, advanced technology. This "engineering man" can be overridden by the "economic man" when price competition is the rule. But when the firm has a monopolistic advantage, the engineering man seems to be allowed to override the economic man. Indeed, a capital-intensive plant might be able to respond more quickly to fluctuations in demand, upward or downward, than a labour-intensive plant. This insurance coverage seems to underlie many managers feeling that capital-intensive plants are "cheaper in the long run". But only the firms that have a monopolistic position can afford to pay the insurance premium in the form of higher production costs.

As for the very labour-intensive firms, Wells finds quite a few cases where even the economic man could endorse the use of more capital to replace labour. For example, the annual wages of cigarette rollers run on the order of ₡100 per year. A shift from hand rolling to machine rolling requires, according to his calculation, an incremental investment of no more than ₡50 to ₡120 per worker saved. Even at 36 per cent interest rate (plus 10 per cent depreciation), this implies an annual capital cost of only ₡26 to ₡55 per worker saved. Hand rolling continues, however, because of the unavailability of capital even at that interest rate, because the differential excise tax favours hand-rolled cigarettes, and because there still exists a local market that prefers hand-rolled cigarettes. In most of the instances where the shift from very labour-intensive to "intermediate" classes of technology appeared an economically attractive proposition, the unavailability of the required capital for the particular entrepreneurs at almost any price is said to be acting as a dominant constraint. The situation at this end of the gamut of the LDC dual economy thus resembles the classical case in development economics.

In concluding his highly illuminating case study, Wells expresses his impression that the conflict between the economic man and the engineering man has been, if any, much less serious in the advanced countries; he even attempts to put forward a hypothesis that the range of alternative technologies that operate side by side in a country is an increasing function of the labour-capital price ratio prevailing in that country. Although this impression is not too unreasonable, something more needs to be said since the coexistence of old and new technologies is not a unique phenomenon in LDCs. In fact, the history of modern technological evolution abounds in examples of the competitive survival of less modern technologies along with more modern ones, the diffusion of the latter being normally an extremely time-consuming process. There have been many new inventions which are no better prepared than DC modern plants just transplanted into LDCs to convert themselves into events of full economic significance. An invention needs many other supplementary inventions, technical skills and economic and institutional developments before it becomes a commercially viable innovation. If we get very particular about the process of real assimilation, adaptation and diffusion of new technology, those quasi-economic operations based on imported technology in LDCs, if lucky enough to be given a monopolistic position for survival, may have to be considered only as an event of R and D significance. How fast can the adaptation process be? Let us recall, with the help of John L. Enos[1], that there was a lag as long as 53 years between Angus Campbell's first conception of a spindle-type cotton picker (in 1889) and the first commercial application of that invention (in 1942); television took 22 years after an invention dated 1919; flourescent lamps 79 years (invention dated 1859); gyro-compass 56 years (invention dated 1852); etc.

Nathan Rosenberg directs our attention to the fact that the "old" technology continues to be improved after the introduction of the "new" - an important factor accounting for the slowness of the technology diffusion[2]. For example, water wheels had undergone a number of important improvements before the stationary steam engine was established as a new power source in the first half of the 19th century; the introduction of water turbines after 1840 reduced the cost of water power, and the steam power accounted for only 51.8 per cent of primary-power capacity in the U.S. manufacture even as late as 1869, having affected primarily locations where water power sources were unavailable and fuel was easily available. With the rise of the iron hull cargo steamship in the

1) John L. Enos, The Rate and Direction of Inventive Activity, Princeton University Press, 1962, pp. 307-308.
2) Nathan Rosenberg, "Factors Affecting the Diffusion of Technology" in Explorations in Economic History, Autumn 1972, Vol. 10, No. 1, pp. 23-28.

1850s, the wooden sailing ship underwent various imaginative changes, including the use of an iron skeleton for its hull, the doubling of cargo space relative to tonnage, the modifications of sails and rigging to reduce crew requirements, etc; thus even in the 1870s, the sailing ship was still functioning as the chief replenisher of overseas coaling bases and depots. Rosenberg suggests that inter-technological competition and the asymmetries in the manner in which business firms respond to changes in their profit prospects, can perhaps contribute to improvements in overall industrial efficiency more than other more diffuse pressures of intra-industry competition.

It is not clear whether one can stretch this observation so far as to say that the continual improvements of old technologies providing close substitutes should be regarded as a "necessary" condition for successful self-improvements and diffusion of new inventions. But history abounds in evidence that the conception of technological advancement as an intermittent and discontinuous phenomenon is simply inadequate. And still more important is that inter-breeding between new and old technologies, that accompanies the process of technology diffusion, does not take place overnight. Today, many LDCs clearly recognise that the technology transferred to them by DC industrialists and experts is, as a rule, not adapted to the conditions of their own countries; it has not become permeable into their society yet; so their own indigenous sector and the actual system of technology underlying it need greater attention. Perhaps, without active efforts to bring about continual improvements in indigenous technology, there would be little pressure for truly adaptive assimilation of foreign technology.

Chapter VI

SCIENCE AND INDUSTRY : INTERFACE MECHANISMS AND POLICY OBJECTIVES

Marc Chapdelaine (UNESCO) was invited to inform the Group of the gist of the method being employed by UNESCO for the preparation and formulation of science policy in developing countries. He addressed himself specifically to the problem of the interaction between science policy and development policy in individual countries. The relative isolation of scientific communities from those more directly involved in economic activities has been found to be a common disease of practically all the developing countries examined. (Frankly, few would say that this is only the case with developing countries!) Consequently, the very first problem to be tackled is how to improve the ability of scientists to evaluate the social and economic implications of their own trade.

Economists from planning agencies, too, tend to neglect the potential contribution of scientists to the process of formulating economic plans. In the short-run planning context, the consequences of a failure in inter-disciplinary communication may not be too obvious. However, in a long-term context it will simply imply the absence of any meaningful framework of long-term development planning.

In order to bridge the gap, a dialogue must be established between the two communities: producers of research and scientific manpower on the one hand, and users of the research results and manpower on the other. The methodology of UNESCO science policy assistance is thus concerned with structuring such a dialogue. By way of "needs" analysis, a language has been introduced in the operations research style. In short, the UNESCO method consists in constructing a matrix of "relevance marks" whereby a number of disciplinary fields of research and training are evaluated against a set of identified development goals. The goals will be ranked and weighted (although this often proves itself a painful exercise). Adding relevance marks gives the composite relevance of each discipline for all identified goals. With estimates of the capability in each discipline, this information may then be used to guide planners and scientists in spotting critical needs and formulating appropriate institutional policies and programmes.

This method has been applied in a certain number of developing countries, mostly African and Latin American. In application, it is necessary to bring together members from both the scientific communities and the planning agencies. The confrontation reveals many conflicts. Fortunately, many of the apparent conflicts are observed to have originated from purely semantic ambiguities. Dispelling such ambiguities, the method has proved capable of forcing a reconciliation of subjective assessments in terms of relevance marks. The exercise has always proved a most fruitful educational exercise for both scientists and planners in working out some common language - an absolute prerequisite for the integration of science and economic policies.

Chapdelaine did not hesitate to point out that the method is fraught with many difficulties in actual application. The major one is said to be the lack of familiarity with the approach and language of operations research, very often on the part of planners. Another is the lack of details in the statement of develop ment goals: statements given by planners are often not in terms that are directly interpretable by scientists. Very often, the planner's operational targets are stated in terms of "products", such as rice, maize, newsprint, cement, etc. in such and such quantities, rather than in terms of development programmes, such as irrigation, urban housing, etc. The SITC and even the ISIC do not always coincide with the disciplinary language with which scientists evaluate the relevance of their trade.

When considered against the immense complexity of interaction between science policy and economic policy, the UNESCO exercise as described above is quite modest both in its objective and its scope. Its objective may be said to consist in stimulating, almost in the "starting-from-scratch" fashion, thinking towards "partici-patory" planning and policy decisions. The latter process is very heuristic in nature, and (despite its crucial importance for the realities of society facing developmental activities at all levels), very little is established by way of general methodology and con-vention to act upon this process. On that score, the exercise is well intended. But the idea of setting up an ad hoc arena for confrontation between different disciplinary professions may sound surprisingly simplistic. It would invite many questions: among others -

i)   who defines the development goals?

ii) apart from establishing specific technical objectives
     for research and training, how can we examine mechanisms
     that affect the orientation of scientific efforts both
     collectively and individually?

Suppose that the arena were represented by only two profes-sions, scientists and economic planners. One would normally expect some more serious gaps between them than a mere language barrier. Economists can work efficiently in making projections and policy analyses under the assumption of constant technology. On the other hand, scientists in general might feel more competent in projecting consequences of the autonomous developments in pure science under the assumption that the economic society should be able to adapt

itself somehow to these consequences. The relevance of one trade
for the other can thus be a matter for mutual questioning. In
defining development goals and objectives, it would indeed be a
useful exercise to attempt to subordinate science to economy, at
least at the beginning. In the LDC situation where the existing
R and D base is small and resources available for its development
are extremely scarce, this approach is in fact imperative. In the
case of the OECD policy studies initiated around 1963 in the less
developed member countries, too, the point of departure for the
Pilot Staff was to make clearly visible, in each country considered, the overall strategy of economic development and the major
constraints and bottlenecks to be taken into account in defining
priority fields of science and technology. Subsequently, however,
the development strategy itself could be questioned and corrected
on the basis of the expected outputs from their specific programmes
envisaged in the various fields and their implications in terms of
basic technological constraints facing the economy.

Among the more industrialised OECD countries, there has
recently been growing attention to the question of the "mechanism"
or social-behavioural pattern whereby the national R and D industry is linked to various national goals. Apart from (perhaps)
exceptionally successful cases in the field of nuclear energy and
aerospace, the necessary or possible objectives have often proved
shifting and elusive. When government R and D policy is turned
into political issues, the list of specific social functions and
objectives with which the policy inputs (e.g. government R and D
expenditures) are to be associated will become diversified as
different interest groups get involved in the examination; moreover,
the relative priorities given to various functions and objectives
will vary greatly from one group to another (e.g. a "right" wing
would give higher priorities to such objectives as defence and
industrial production while a "left" wing would emphasise more
such objectives as environment, social planning and welfare). The
complex social communication system linking the individuals and
groups which make up the "national R and D policy community" thus
constitutes an important concept. In describing R and D policy as
a social innovation process(1), Stevan Didijer (University of Lund)
wishes to include in the policy community all the people who are

---

1) S. Didijer, "National R and D policy as a social innovation",
   in Management of Research and Development, OECD, 1972,
   pp. 93-109.

concerned with the development and/or use of the R and D industry, any one of its sectors, or any aspects of them. They constitute various "R and D policy congeries" or sub-communities. Some are members of central science policy organs such as National Committee on Science and Technology or National Research Council; the members of the Atomic Energy Commission, the Defense Research Administration, University Research Administration, etc. may also be included among the primary policy congeries. There are also people who serve on advisory panels of these bodies and thus have a secondary R and D policy role, while their primary role is in industrial firms, specialised research institutes or universities. Those who participate in R and D policy discussions in a less formal fashion, express their views in professional forums and produce information for other R and D policy men, can also be said to form the tertiary congeries. These different congeries can be further classified according to specific branches of R and D, industrial, agricultural, meteorological, defense, etc. The healthiness of a country's R and D policy might then be measured in terms of the proportion of the total population which belongs to at least one of the congeries within the total R and D community.

Admittedly, Didijer's thought as above is perhaps too loosely formulated to stand as a practical methodology for policy science. Some might stretch a similar discussion in terms of "centralisation versus spontaneity", or "fragmented institution-building efforts versus the generation of a mechanism liable for continual and reciprocal links between science and industry", etc. In the Western European countries, government intervention in science and research activities has traditionally been a matter of successive "nudges" rather than the direct imposition of order and authority. As George Ferné says, one of its consequences has been that different generations of institutions exist now alongside one another, thus inevitably making the research mechanism more cumbersome and again raising the problem of choice between "centralism and spontaneity"(1). In the case of most LDCs the situation appears totally different. There is yet no attempt nor capability on the part of domestic industrialists to undertake R and D on their products which were in the first instance produced with imported know-how. The R and D laboratories set up by governments have often drifted towards open-ended research problems, the choice of which reflect the voluntary

_____

1) G. Ferné, "In Search of a Policy" in the Research System, Vol. I (France, Germany, U.K.) OECD, 1972, p.45.

orientation and interests of the laboratory directors and scientists. The "green revolution" pursued by the Council of Agricultural Research in India may be among the exceptional cases. Laboratories associated with the user ministries, in the hope of tightening the laboratory-industry linkage, are found in many instances to have been no more effective than the laboratories associated with an autonomous research organisation like the Indian Council of Scientific and Industrial Research (CSIR)(1).

The CSIR in India attempted to apply various alternative methods for drawing up its planning framework: social merit matrix model, discipline matrix model, sectoral emphasis matrix model, etc. In any one of these methods, the weighting factors to be assigned to various socio-economic objectives defined in one form or another emerged as a decisive element for the allocation of research resources, and no simple procedures are yet available to cope with this decisive element. The Committee of Science and Technology of the Government of India thus noted, at the Third National Conference of Scientists, Technologists and Educationalists, (November 1970), that R and D policy gaps in fact represented gaps in the information available for R and D planning, for the evaluation of technologies actually in use, and for gaining closer grips with the pattern and structure of R and D activities in the country. And as to the last factor, one of the most painful findings was that the dialogue between industry and R and D establishments in the country, which is the obvious necessity for fully exploiting the outputs of the latter, could not be very meaningful in the absence of in-house R and D capability with industry itself.

If anyone wished to resort to the Erich Jantsch type of heavy words, the core of the question raised above might be tantamount to pointing to the need for a real science policy that would be capable to develop organisation forms ensuring "gaining flexibility by acting from inside existing structures"(2). While this is a matter of equally serious concern to both DCs and LDCs, there are not infrequent indications that, given equally conscious efforts, the relatively young vintage of LDC institutional structures

1) S.R. Valluri, "Mobilisation of National Resources and Planning of Industrial Research and Development", UNIDO, ID/WG.132/10, October 1972.

2) See esp. E. Jantsch: "From Forecasting and Planning to Policy Science", in Management of Research and Development (op.cit), pp. 139-159.

would permit a higher degree of flexibility towards the re-culturation of industry-science links. The research and training institutions in LDCs, once proliferated by replicating various DC models, did not take much time to prove their own deficiencies in face of real local requirements. The pressure of resource scarcity is often strong enough to overwhelm that of inertia in he policy decisions of national and international funding agencies. In fact, a newly emerging trend in the institution-building policy in LDCs seems to be more for re-organisation and consolidation of existing scattered facilities than for juxta-position of new facilities along with old ones.

Helpful as it is, "gaining flexibility" is not by itself a solution. Science-industry links mean much broader and far-reaching tasks in the case of LDCs than in the case of DCs. Re-deployment of the already available skills and talents (and introducing new order and consistency into the existing institutional complexities) is perhaps only a minor aspect of the total linkage problem for LDCs. Skills and talents have to be brought up anew, as well as professors and trainers qualified for such a task. Curricula and teaching materials too have to be re-developed to suit the needs of local industries. All these would not be possible without properly institutionalised linkage between the university and the industry communities. And to the extent that industry is not very much counted on for initiative-taking in this direction much think-ing and action will have to be done on the part of those who are to undertake "think-tank" activities in and around the university community.

Chapter VII

TECHNOLOGY ASSESSMENT : ANY LESSONS TO BE LEARNED

"Technology Assessment" does not sound like a very new idea if interpreted in a literal fashion. The workers' revolt against machines during the Industrial Revolution, the clinical testing of pharmaceutical products, or even the benefit-cost analysis of developmental projects might all be said to involve an element of technology assessment in one form or another. Indeed, the term has been given sudden legitimacy and urgency under the anti-pollution crusades of today; emphasis has thus been given to un-intended indirect and delayed effects of technology on society. But what gives a new, special meaning to technology assessment is perhaps the fact that this art of evaluation represents the effort to grip "technology" as an object of direct policy control at the governmental level. That is, in the terminology of Robert W. Lamson, "control", in addition to "perception" and "evaluation", consti-tutes a crucially important phase of technology assessment in the today's sense of the term.

Historically, the term in this special sense emerged first (in 1967) with Emilio Q. Daddario, as an expression of U.S. Congressional concern about the need for a more systematic analy-sis of the impact of modern technology on society. While the legis-lation in the U.S. to establish an Office of Technology Assessment is still pending (a somewhat narrower version, "National Environ-mental Policy Act" was enacted as of January 1st, 1970), the idea of establishing technology assessment as a policy instrument has quickly spread to most advanced countries. The growing official interest of the OECD Member countries in the subject was reflected by the Seminar on Technology Assessment convened in Paris, 26th-28th January, 1972. Generally speaking, however, the less developed nations have shown a lesser degree of enthusiasm about the idea. This is perhaps partly due to its more or less direct association with the environment question, and partly on account of the popu-larity of other terms such as transfer of technology, appropriate technology, adaptations of technology, etc. that appear to be good enough to express the LDC concern about their technology problems. Is there anything noteworthy in the latest developments in tech-nology assessment methodology that would be relevant for LDC technology policies? Would any part of the currently available methodology help elaborate models for choice of technology or a framework in which alternatives and adaptation possibilities are to be identified and appraised in the LDC context?

Glenn Schweitzer, who had produced an exploratory article on a similar subject(1) at a U.S. AID Seminar several months earlier was invited to reflect upon this question. The study commissioned

---

1) Glenn Schweitzer, "Towards a Methodology for Assessing the Impact of Technology in Developing Countries", now available in Technology and Economics in International Development, Washington, D.C., AID, May 1972.

to the Mitre Corporation by the U.S. Office of Science and Technology (in the Executive Office of the President) was intended to
develop a general methodology for technology assessment. For that
purpose, five pilot studies were undertaken, covering automotive
products' role in air pollution, the impact on society of computer-
communication network, technological trends in the enzyme industry,
applications of mariculture in LDCs, and water pollution from
domestic wastes, respectively.

These studies addressed such questions as:

  i)   Where does the technology currently stand?

 ii)   In what direction does it seem to be developing?

iii)   In what way is the technology likely to be applied?

 iv)   What factors are likely to influence that application?

  v)   What are the likely secondary and tertiary consequences
       of the application?

 vi)   What benefits and costs are likely to accrue from public
       efforts to alter either the technology applications or
       their subsequent consequences?

vii)   Which community or interest groups are most likely to
       be affected by the anticipated impacts of the technolog-
       ical applications and are most likely to take action to
       influence those impacts?

It goes without saying that there hardly exists a unique
methodology generally agreed upon for conducting the comprehensive
analyses needed to answer such questions. While the questions themselves are no novelty, a comprehensive analytical treatment of them
would be almost a super-human task - like the question of how to
eat an elephant, as Professor Raymond Bauer once remarked. But the
Mitre Study did not hesitate to point to the fact that, these questions being the ones which have long been asked in various disciplinary fields, this is certainly the opportunity for developing
articulated uses of the various analytical techniques which have
so far emerged in separate fields of specialisation. Operations
research, benefit-cost analysis, cost effectiveness analysis, systems analysis, management science, computer simulation, PPBS, policy
science, etc., can all be mobilised to build up the necessary joint
study capability. Thus, instead of the single-numeraire type of
approach, one has to seek an evaluation method based on multi-

dimensional criteria, or a merger of economics, sociology and
engineering sciences. In addition, politics, law, administration,
etc. ought to step in to deal with the question of institutional
practicability of technically plausible solutions.

Schweitzer seemed to want to express the same philogophy,
but presumably he was not quite convinced of the utility for LDCs
of such esoteric tools as multi-purpose matrix and computer simulation. Consequently, he preferred an approach that can most generally be described as:

    i) checklists and
   ii) case studies (or post audits).

This is hardly a rigorous methodology; it does not even
suggest any special principles or techniques according to which
to draw up a checklist and conduct a case study. But in the world
of practical reality, he prefers letting the methodological generalisation stop at that; he would rather point to the need for
separate methodologies tailored to the conditions in different
countries, and to different types of technology or activity, such
as heavy manufacturing, light manufacturing, power construction,
etc.

The possibly interesting interface between technology assessment methodology and technology policy issues in LDCs did not seem
to be explored sufficiently in Schweitzer's article. For one thing,
his attention was directed rather exclusively to the problem of
imported technologies, involving mainly engineering technologies,
on which an LDC government is to make some deliberate decisions,
some other key issues were not considered. Again, in an effort to
be practical, he assumed that LDC policy decision makers' interest
in the assessment of the impact of technology would be primarily
limited to decisions with a lead time of no more than 3 to 5 years -
"long enough to weigh options seriously but not so long as to be
unrealistic". He was thus afraid of the possibility that too serious an assessment effort might result in "technology arrestment",
as the environmentalists in advanced countries are often inclined
to do. While technology assessment is generally concerned with the
second and higher order effects of technology choice and innovation,
he anticipated that for LDCs the direct effects would be generally
much more important. If this is actually the case with those concerned with LDC technology policies, it does not necessarily follow
that such preoccupations need not be contested, however.

What is not very clear in the foregoing discussion is precisely what is meant by "technology" in general. Without some basic
taxonomy in which to locate the various systems, sub-systems, components, material and processes appearing in the discussion of
technological substitutions a degree of semantic anarchy would be
unavoidable. To speak of "methods of production" in general,
referring to "everything concerned with and arising from production
in an economy", as Frances Stewart put it(1), would not help draw
any map for our travel amid the enormous complexities of the
technological landscape. To the extent that we believe that technological change is not so much driven by autonomous scientific
discoveries and inventions as by the changing awareness of human
and social needs, a taxonomy of technological events may be started
by exploring some kind of "normative" framework whereby evolving
social needs can be related to possibilities.

In the technology circle, there are certain accepted ways
of distinguishing one field of specialisation from another. In
terms of functional characteristics technology systems related to
structural properties (or static configurations) may be so distinguished from those related to mechanical properties (dynamic
configurations); similarly, technological events concerning thermal properties, electrochemical and nuclear conversion, optical
and visual properties, acoustic and auditory properties, fluid
properties, etc. can be so isolated. Important is to note that
some sort of "substitution ladder" can be conceived for each of
such functional fields. The ladder will have several levels: the
system level, the subsystem level, the component level, and the
material level. At each level, various competing types may be
identified so that substitution possibilities open at one level
can be linked to those open at the next level. For example, substitutions involving thermal properties may be examined with
reference to a number of engine-machine systems (heat engine with
torque output, heat engine with jet output, space-heating system,
space-cooling system, high-temperature heat storage and generation
systems, etc.); for each of these systems (e.g. heat engine, jet
output) one can find several competing types (e.g. turbo-jet, ram-
jet, rocket). At the level of engine-machine sub-systems (burners,
combustion chambers, radiative-convective heat exchangers - low
and high temperatures separately - ignition, etc.), the known

---

1) See Chapter I, page 113 of this review.

competing types for burners are, for example, simple, vortex, and
double vortex. At the next level, basic thermal components such
as metal burner parts, temperature-resistant structural elements,
thermal conducting elements, hot and cold insulators, salts for
heat-of-fusion storage, etc., identifiable competing materials
will be stainless steel, nickel-chrome super alloy, carbon steel,
aluminium, copper, glas., asbestos, ceramics, plastics, etc.(1)

The question is, however, how far one can go up this type
of substitution ladder. The "system" level reached in the above
reflection is yet at a high level of specificity, perhaps still
too remote from the sort of questions of public concern in the
context of technology assessment. Thus, an alternative way for
building substitution ladders may be "from the top down", instead
of "from the bottom up". But a normative thinking towards generalised concepts of goals would entail an element of heroism in one
way or another. Robert Ayres, for example, proposes a set of three
basic goals (at the highest level of macro-system substitution
ladder):

    a) survival-growth of individual (both physical and
         psychological terms)

    b) survival-growth of community/nation, and

    c) intellectual and spiritual growth.

A one step more concrete version is then spelled out referring to "contributory goals" such as

    a) personal space, air, water and food, protection from
         hazard and disease, protection of economic and psychic
         status at the level of individual),

    b) political order, social and economic order, economic
         production and growth, international order, military
         power (at the level of community/nation) and

    c) education, science, arts, recreation, religion (goals
         not explicitly included in the above two levels).

One step further down in the ladder, more specific categories
of "final" and "intermediate" services may be identified. It is

---

1) These examples related to the taxonomy of technological sub-
    stitutions owe to Robert Ayres (International Research and
    Technology Corporation, Washington, D.C.) who was good enough
    to show us a relevant part of his working draft on this subject.

important to note that in the context of technology assessment, many of these categories flow out of the frontier of SITC or any other conventional categories of "economic" needs and activities. That is, personal territory, personal mobility, air protection, ecological protection, ability to communicate, protection of civic rights, ability to locate natural resources, resource conservation, manipulation of biochemical processes, manipulation of social relations, etc. would emerge explicitly in the typology of services/functions serving the contributory goals. The next logical step is to identify alternative strategic possibilities for providing each functional service: e.g. for birth control, competing strategies are chemical, surgical, endocrine, and bio-feedback possibilities. There will then be alternative systems concepts to be identified as being appropriate for each strategy: e.g. for the surgery system, competing possibilities will include cryogenics, scalpel, ultrasonic drill, and laser. In the functional field of bio-medical engineering there will be, further, substitution possibilities at the sub-system level referring to those directly affecting cells rather than organs: e.g. cloning and tissue culture offer possibilities open for asexual reproduction.

While the methodology is indeed straightforward, the richness of alternatives conceived at the various levels might easily lead to an infinite proliferation of the taxonomical possibilities. Another major difficulty would be that such a morphological search and the map resulting thereof ought to be further treated anatomically. In particular, inter-dependencies among the separated contributory goals and among the various functional services would need further analytical formulations in order to permit reasonable weighting of the alternative strategic possibilities. The techniques of input-output analysis developed within the field of economics might find some applications there, but a complete structural analysis with multiple goals and with combined use of the tool-boxes of different disciplines would certainly be an enormous task. But from the above example, it will become clear that technology assessment is only a newly opening field, its boundaries being yet unfixed. The various specific exercises actually undertaken so far in the DC context might not immediately take us very far along the current LDC preoccupations about the choice and adaptation of technology. But the movement in this new field should be considered as a challenge to the conventional policy framework of economic growth. The challenge is of such a fundamental nature that it will only precipitate our search for a clearer planning and policy framework of "technology and development" for LDCs as well.

Chapter VIII

MEASUREMENT OF TECHNOLOGICAL DEVELOPMENT

The reconciliation of micro- and macro-analysis has long
been a thorny problem in economics. "Planning and policy appraisals" could mean different things for different people - not only
with respect to their disciplinary implications, but also with
respect to the levels to which they refer within the hierarchical
structure of policy action. Some are concerned with economy-wide
problems; some with sector or branch levels; and some with project
or individual activity unit levels. Data used by economists, or
by those concerned with behavioural characteristics of the society,
are usually in the form of "statistics". Statistics are susceptible
to aggregation and disaggregation with various criteria of relevance for given analytical purposes. Can technology be treated in
the same way?

For a macro-economic analyst, technology is usually considered as either something that is embodied in the factors of production (labour and capital) or something that affects the input-
output relationships. Whichever way it may be handled, little
attempt has been made to go any farther than the kind of typology
that refers to economic characteristics of technology such as
capital-using, labour-saving, capital-saving, labour-using, neutral,
etc. In fact, these terms are not meant to describe technology per
se, but they describe only the behaviour of factor proportions
associated with the use of technology.

If this constitutes one extremity, "technologists" emerge
at the other extremity. Technology is represented by this and that
specific way of doing things. If you want to know about drilling
in the machine-tool industry, for example, technologists can tell
you that drilling consists of cutting, enlarging or finishing a
round hole, which can be performed by some cutting tool, either
single drill or multiple drill; the nature of the job varies so
that drilling in general covers boring, reaming and honing, etc.
But if you want to know the basic technology of the machine-tool

industry, you should also know about lathing, milling, planing, grinding, forming, welding, etc. Sugar refinery? For that, some other technologists will tell you how sugar cane is milled, clarified, filtered, evaporated, boiled, centrifuged, dried, etc; but there are three basic systems available for the boiling operation: the vacuum pan process, the Khandsari or open-pan sulphitation process, and the jaggery process; and your choice in this respect will affect other operations a little; etc.

Listening to technologists, economists are inevitably impressed that technology as such requires an understanding of ways of doing a great many different things, each viewed at a super-micro level. (Note that in economic statistics the micro-data refer to no smaller activity unit than a "firm" or an "establishment", which is almost too complex an enormity for technologists.) Since ISIC has not reached that level (in fact not even the possibility, nor the plausibility, of doing so has ever been discussed seriously), planning economists have contributed very little to the way in which technology can be treated as an integral part of their planning methodology.

Today, the people concerned with questions of scientific and technological planning seem to think that "technology" consists of a set of sectors and sub-sectors, which can be related more or less directly to given needs or goals of the society. Some argue that, at any given time, the sectors of technology must be in balance in terms of creating and satisfying needs; in other words, each sector's input either satisfies a need directly or is required as an input to other co-existing technological sectors. This argument clearly points to an analogy with the economists' "input-output" framework. How to select a set of technological sectors depends indeed on how to define the social needs or goals to which they are related. If social needs are defined in terms of the Leontief final demand vector, the matching definition of technology sectors may not be very much different from the Leontief matrix. But, without getting involved with the production-function type of formulation, technologists tend to have their own ways of selecting the parameters characterising each technology sector.

For example, for the satisfaction of the need for food, an agricultural technology may be represented by a set of technology sectors, such as:

   i)   agronomy,
  ii)   agricultural chemicals; and
 iii)   agricultural machinery and equipment.

As the major input sectors to these, one would further add,

iv) machine tools; and

v) power.

Examining the historical development of each sector in an advanced country, one may then attempt to identify successive stages of technical evolution; e.g. in the case of agricultural chemicals, the U.S. history may be viewed in terms of the following four distinctive development stages(1):

Stage 1: (Before 1900): small scale batch manufacture; super-phosphate from phosphate ores; nitrogen as purified natural sodium nitrate; potassium from wood ash.

Stage 2: (1900-1930): large scale batch manufacture; super-phosphate from phosphate ores treated with sulphuric acid from Frasch process sulphur; nitrogen from nitrogen fixation by calcium carbide; potassium from minerals.

Stage 3: (1930-1950): large scale continuous processing; super-phosphate and potassium as above; nitrogen by direct fixation (Haber process).

Stage 4: (Current): fertilisers as above; large scale production of other agricultural chemicals such as pesticides, fungicides and herbicides.

In the case of machine tools, practically all the basic machine tool designs were completed by 1850. Subsequent improvements were achieved by such inventions as:

- the Colt revolver (1849-1854) and gauges by Root which added to the principle of the manufacture of standardised components;

- Mushet's discovery (around 1868) of tungsten, vanadium and manganese to be introduced into tool steel, which increased cutting speed from about 40 feet/minute (with simple carbon steel) to 120 feet/minute;

- the Norton gear box in 1892 which improved the cutting speed adjustment system;

---

1) See e.g. A Methodology for Planning Technological Development, report to UNESCO by Arthur D. Little, Inc., and Hetrick Associates, Inc., (September, 1970).

- incorporation of electric motors (around 1920);

- development of the new concept of automation from around
  1950, with the numerically controlled machine tool.

By availing oneself of a series of logistic curves expressing
the evolving technical efficiency of each sector, one may attempt
to build a framework of appraisal of each country's status of
scientific and technological development for given types of need.
Can one then establish a coherent system of measurement of the
national technological capability, that could be used parallel to
the economist's national account system and thus would be of more
direct help for scientific and technological planning and policy?
Indeed, the long tradition with our educational and training
routines has brought about an intelligible and sensible system of
classification and quality grading in the field of basic science.
However, technology is a more intractable problem, if viewed from
within the economic and industrial activities to which it is
applied, than from within the basic and applied scientific activities from which it emanates; our knowledge of its classificatory
characteristics seems rather disorderly, if abundant. Is the question too esoteric? No attempt to ever consider such a question is
known to exist in UNIDO, for example. To try to do one's best in
finding solutions on each narrowly specified technical question is
one thing. But setting relative priorities and targets for efforts
in different disciplinary fields, i.e. technological planning is
another - certainly no less important from the practical standpoint.
UNESCO has devoted some attention to this latter question.
According to Chapdelaine, UNESCO's two-year long exploration
in this field has been making progress rather slowly due to many
dead-ends that have emerged. Its main concern is in the problem of
measurement of STD (Scientific and Technological Development) and
construction of some typological indexes that can help assess the
relative STD positions of different LDCs and thus contribute to
long-term planning techniques. The research has not yet been quite
completed. But the empirical consideration of as many facets of
the STD notion as are deemed relevant has led to a selection and
grouping of certain concepts, and of corresponding indicators when-
ever possible. The entire list now comprises about 125 indicators
under the following broad categories:

   i) indicators of the level of socio-economic development:
       - production system
       - social system

ii) anthropological, organisational and capacity indicators
of "permeability" which are related to the phenomena
having a direct bearing upon STD;

iii) technological indicators (proper):
they relate to the most important technological sectors
or systems (agriculture, transport, energy, plus a few
others), and are divided roughly into two distinctive
groups -

- those indicators which characterise the sectors or the
systems themselves ("intrinsic" characteristics in
terms of physical performances such as the amount of
chemical fertilisers used per acre, kilo-tons of railway traffic per habitant, etc.);

- systems characteristics as observed in different
societal contexts ("extrinsic" characteristics in terms
of diffusion, such as the proportion of single-line
railway in use, etc.).

iv) indicators of scientific and technological potentials,
in terms of human resources, financial resources, information resources, etc.

The readily available data from international and national
statistical yearbooks are being utilised extensively. The current
exercise based on these sources for 34 countries covers more than
80 per cent of the world GNP and population. The present phase of
the research concentrates on making the data on most intrinsic
determinants of STD as complete as possible and correlating them
with the indicators of socio-economic development. In the coming
two years, an effort will be made to finalise the selection of
indicators and to prepare test cases in some developing countries
to find out to what extent such a comprehensive and aggregated
quantitative description of the STD can be used in the actual planning process at the national level.

While the Study Group did not have an opportunity to debate
on Chapdelaine's presentation directly, there was, later, an exchange of views on this matter between him and one author of this
report. It might not be too much of an injustice to him if we understood that his exercise consisted in the main of an effort to re-
align a great number of indicators as available in the conventional
type of statistical yearbooks and to re-interpret their meaningful-
ness in terms of measure of STD. The statistics included seem to

be mostly the kind that measure the intensity of utilisation of goods and services; thus technology is gripped in terms of the performance characteristics of its outputs delivered into economic life. Chapdelaine's distinction between "intrinsic" and "extrinsic" does not quite coincide with normal distinctions between technology and economy. Besides, the entire basket covers indicators of socio-economic development, human, financial and information resources, etc. This would immediately remind us of those various attempts made by development economists to assemble a number of statistical quantities and ratios relevant for the measurement of welfare effects of development.

To the extent that the UNESCO basket is a variant of the compendium of development statistics, the problem of index number, or more specifically the problem of finding appropriate weights for aggregative assessment will re-emerge. The question is: are we interested in a collection of quantities to be compared or in prices that help compare such quantities? If information on various quantities(1) individually is all of the well known (and readily available) kind, the real merit of the exercise should lie precisely in a special way of combining them. Our impression is that Chapdelaine's research has not yet settled this question in an explicit way.

Now, reverting to our original question, we are interested in appraising the distance between a nation's use of technology-intensive commodities and its ability to assimilate that technology for creative application. For example, the gap between national steel consumption and steel production needs to be treated properly in measuring the successfulness of technology transfer in a given country. Furthermore, even steel production by itself cannot necessarily represent the country's technological ability to produce steel; it has to be supplemented by an indication of the import dependency in terms of process technologies and know-how. Data on R and D will thus eventually occupy a key position in the entire set of indicators. As Chapdelaine himself pointed out, however, many LDCs are still at a stage where the very concept of R and D has not gained an institutional base clear enough for meaningful statistical assessment. Apparently, a more imaginative system of appraisal is needed to grasp their technological "capability" from their actual ways of doing things, of which "R and D" in the formal sense of the term constitute only a marginal proportion.

---

1) Various component indicators in the UNESCO case.

Suppose that we move down to the level of individual industrial firms and try to assess their aptitude to assimilate technology. Technology in its narrow sense that refers to production techniques alone may not be adequate for the purpose. In reporting on the Istanbul Seminar on Transfer of Technology(1), E.P. Hawthorne emphasised the concept of "elements of technology". These elements can lie in a number of fields of activity within the firms, such as research, design, material, production, marketing, general management, etc. Generally speaking, the key elements of technology vary from industry to industry, but broadly cover the following:

i) the nature of the product's performance required by the customer's technology, which highlights the kind of design know-how to be incorporated in the product;

ii) methods of manufacture, with regard to materials, process designs, methods for quality and reliability, etc;

iii) market control, including such factors as:
   - matching of product range with intended market;
   - knowledge of competitors' development;
   - appraisal of likely changes in customers needs and buying mechanisms;

iv) infrastructure or supply networks necessary to back up the product type and in-house manufacturing capability.

Applying this thought to the Portuguese machine tool industry, Hawthorne identified six elements of technology:

   - metal characteristics
   - customer product characteristics;
   - metal working process characteristics;
   - process support infrastructure;
   - market control;
   - machine tool technology.

One might elaborate a detailed checklist for evaluating the level of development or aptitude for each of these elements. But, with the instinct of "management consultants", he seems to feel able to give some ratings in such terms as:

---

1) The Seminar held in Istanbul, 5th-9th October 1970, under the aegis of the OECD. A report on the Seminar is included in: Edward P. Hawthorne, The Transfer of Technology, Paris (OECD), 1971.

A : comprehensive control exercised;

B : partial control;

C : some but insufficient control;

D : little or no control.

It is not clear how different assessors can give consistent ratings without defining specific parameters to be measured pertaining to the degree of "control". One of the interesting findings from his exercise with the Portuguese machine tool industry is, however, that each firm examined received quite uniform ratings across different elements: i.e. poor cases proved poor with respect to most elements of technology (except that the supply infrastructure was treated as a constant for all firms within given industry). This led Hawthorne to conclude that "no weakness stands out significantly above the remainder, indicating the need to treat technology as a 'system' problem in which a broad front advance is necessary if any worthwhile total result is to be achieved".

This conclusion is somewhat surprising, since it implies that for the purpose of assessment of technological capability one does not have to be particular about different "elements" of technology; one indicator will do for a firm; an "industry" can be represented then by the average value of the same kind of indicator. So far so good. But one will now realise that we are talking about the rating of technological capability rather than technological capability as such. Even without troubling a special technology assessor, we might well be content with the conventional productivity indicators, which tell us no more about the underlying technological features. Then, we have crawled out of just another dead-end.

With the growing concern about international movement of industry and questions of adjustment policy that accompany it, various indicators are being developed to grip differential characteristics of various industrial product lines. Tinbergen's factor proportions are already a well thumb-marked one; "knowledge intensity" is another. While the latter appears to bear more directly upon our concern about technology transfer and adaption, most of its variations attempt to circumvent the possibility of direct perception of 'technology'. An interesting example is the index of relative knowledge-intensity constructed by Mitsui

Information Development Inc. of Japan(1). This draws upon the
four types of factor-intensity index worked out by the Ministry
for International Trade and Industry, and applies the resulting
synthetic index to the detailed classification of manufactures
(about 150 product groups). The index incorporates five criteria:

- income elasticity of demand;
- (historical) rate of increase in productivity;
- environmental density;
- skill content of labour; and
- sources of resource saving.

The synthetic index is derived as the logarithmic mean of
these five index numbers (each being normalised by setting the
observed maximum at unity). The adoption of logarithmic mean
implies emphasis on the synergetic significance of the different
criteria (or the 'system' concept in the case of Hawthorne's
approach cited before).

The resulting picture happens to be somewhat different from
one based on the conventional criterion related to capital intensity. Generally it accords high values to those product lines
subject to high rate of obsolescence in design, high rate of
technical innovations in recent years, and information-intensive
business strategies. 'Applied electronic apparatus' appears at the
top (synthetic index equals 0.821), but other lines of electronic
industry (such as electronic measuring apparatus, electronic parts
for communication equipment, etc.), do not show unexpectedly high
index values. The second highest are newspapers, printing and pub-
lishing (0.700 to 0.720). Bicycles have as high a value as 0.595;
plastic fabrication products 0.627; toys and sporting goods 0.613;
automobiles 0.642; fur and leather coats 0.641. In contrast,
petroleum refinery (0.394), chemical fertilisers (0.435), spinning (0.411), steel making and rolling (0.453), etc., belong to
the lowest quintile.

This is not a place for discussing the specific detail of
this particular system of indicators. But it should be kept in
mind that these indexes have been designed to offer a guidepost
for the contemporary firms in Japan suffering declining business

---

1) Mitsui I.D.I., Association for Machinery Promotion (Centre
for New Machine System), Analysis of the Japanese Industrial
Structure from the Information-knowledge Intensity Viewpoint,
Tokyo, May, 1972, (in Japanese).

and on the lookout for new lines in which to direct their conversion efforts. It indeed remains to be seen if the same set of
criteria when applied to other countries would produce similar
indexes for comparable industries. Some countries might prefer a
different set of criteria if they were to build technology-intensity
indicators to guide their own industries. Chapdelaine's indicators
were oriented toward the search for a broad strategy for scientific
development from the international standpoint. Hawthorne's main
interest was perhaps in re-stressing his theme that technology
needs management(1). There are, and will be, many more indicators
challenging GNP in search of better multidisciplinary planning and
policy tools.

Chapter IX

"MODULES" OF INDUSTRIAL TECHNOLOGY AS A TOOL
FOR ASSIMILATING TECHNICAL INFORMATION

As noted in Chapter VIII, development economics has long
proceeded in a vacuum as far as "technology" is concerned. Even
the "production function" enthusiasts have only bothered about a
number of ways of evaluating the consequences of technological
changes on their economic-behavioural parameters and functions,
instead of converting themselves into technological information
specialists. The Leontief model once appeared to mark a new era
for techno-economics, offering a certain framework, if not the
substance to fill it with, in which the economic structure could
be depicted as being dependent on industry-specific patterns of
technology. Unfortunately, this useful framework stimulated
economic statisticians more than technologists. Perhaps there
still remains a long way for it to reach the level of technologists'
interest. There are many encouraging signs, however, Disaggregation
of input-output tables is increasingly favoured in some countries.

---

1) This theme recurs in many of Hawthorne's writings, e.g.
   "Innovation-oriented Management", paper submitted to the
   CIOS World Congress, Munich, 1972.

In the analysis of technological choice problems, it is recalled that "activity analysis" emerged a few decades ago to challenge the a priori assumption of smooth, continuous isoquants. While the latter is now replaced, for practical programming purposes, by some factual observations on alternative technologies, the number of which is always finite, the basic mathematics and the simplification tactics underlying the optimisation model have permitted its flexible applications to a great variety of cases, rather than propagating the technique of "vestorising" technological information. It had taken some time until the possibility of extending process analysis techniques to industry-wide and economy-wide production systems began to receive economists' attention(1).

When a feasibility study is undertaken on specific investment projects, it is often assumed that project engineers provide a few relevant alternative project designs that are worthy of consideration against given market potential, factor prices, availability of know-how, etc. Whoever prepares such a feasibility study, foreign consultants or potential suppliers of capital equipment, it is usually believed that this is the starting point for the transfer of technology for given specific product lines. Havemann's paper (Background Paper No.3) eloquently described how engineers try to make adjustments to the conditions prevailing in the particular localities considered: quality and price of locally available materials, transport facilities, energy sources, humidity and temperature, etc. If the parties concerned are acquainted only with a limited range of variation possibilities as observed in one or two countries, they naturally tend to make minimum adjustments on what they would establish in those countries. A stronger pressure for thorough adaptation on the part of those who are to receive the information might help widen the margin of adjustments to be effected. Of course, the pressure or negotiation would not work effectively unless it were backed up with some basic knowledge and information of the relevant process technology characteristics as well as with some stimulus for extra adaptation efforts.

"To understand a little bit of technology, you need to understand a whole lot of basic things", remarked M. Sabato. Obvious as it sounds, there is a thorny truth in it. Aggressive assimilation

---

1) See, e.g. A.S. Manne and H.M. Markowitz ed., Studies in Process Analysis - Economy-wide Production Capabilities, 1961. Cowles Foundation Monograph No.18, John Wiley and Sons, Inc., New York; also W. Isard, E.W. Schooler and T. Vietorisz, Industrial Complex Analysis and Regional Development, MIT Press, Cambridge, 1959.

of technology presupposes a degree of basic and applied scientific
capability. Between the process engineering technology as a "commodity of commerce" at one end, and the stock of scientific knowledge as a free good at the other, there lies an almost grey area.
Various institutional policies offer diverse lines for research,
training, information services, etc. Do they have a common map
to follow? As they draw nearer to the commodity of commerce, they
seem to see more mazes than benchmarks. Are there any special ways
of understanding that "whole lot of basic things" that would help
unpack, digest and bring adaptive changes to the commodity of
commerce?

This is perhaps the type of question that José Giral was
asking when he left DuPont after many years experience with the
Company's research and development unit, and embarked on a Mexican
programme for development of appropriate chemical technology(1).
What he calls basic "modules" language for chemical technology
seems to have worked as a special set of benchmarks against which
to cut through the mazy part of the grey area mentioned above.
The language is intentionally more general than the one used in
engineers' process flowsheets; it is rather similar to the language used in the laboratory stage. Instead of swallowing a chain
of numerous specific processes as defined by chemical engineers,
and consequently struggling with the prefixed notion of process
equipment entailed therein, he offers a set of basic modules, such
as chemical transformation, separation of one substance from the
result of the transformation, mixing of that substance with others,
physical transformation into particular sizes and shapes, etc. The
commodity of commerce, usually presented in the form of turn-key
plant, and thus tending to block assimilation efforts with various
apparent and hidden biases, has proved rather easily susceptible
to imaginative unpacking and adaptive innovation, when students
and engineers re-examined it using those basic modules language.
The modules concept permits an open-minded reconsideration of many
laboratory results that were discarded years ago, as well as those
technologies now considered as obsolete by today's major chemical
industrial concerns.

Giral's terminology, "modules", has its own unique connota-
tion. But its orientation is not without precedents and parallels.

---

1) The detail of the programme is presented in Background Paper
   No. 22 and summarised in Part C below.

As early as 1961, an expert group convened by the United Nations[1] placed the concept of "industrial programming data summary" at the front in tackling the basic information problem facing the planning of chemical industries in LDCs. In the context of "preselection" of a development programme for chemical industries, it is not feasible to submit hundreds of potential lines of development to a detailed engineering study or individual project feasibility studies; at this stage, a wide coverage of technological alternatives is essential in order to insure against the risk of overlooking potentially attractive projects. For that purpose, an approximate description of all possible alternatives would be satisfactory. At the same time, the technological data pertaining to specific process designs need to be duly predigested into larger or more general unit process concepts than those of chemical engineers, and preferably in a standardised form, such as the "activity vestor" concept of mathematical programming. This will permit a quick and systematic handling of the enormous amount of computation involved in the evaluation of a large number of alternative processes and process combinations.

The technique of selecting an optimum programme on the basis of the available unit activities makes it essential to separate technological data from pricing information at the outset, and by the same token it is not necessary to limit the data to those technologies currently in use in the industrialised countries; old technology might turn out superior to new technology when placed under some different price and market conditions of non-industrialised countries. A set of 90 reference vectors worthy of consideration for the planning of an acetylene complex, sodium-chloride complex, phosphoric acid complex, etc. were published in the UN Industrialisation and Productivity Bulletin 10, with numerical coefficients based on Thomas Vietorisz' and others' research in the late 1950s[2]. The article emphasised the desirability of installing a special international staff to update and expand continually a similar type of pre-investment data files.

---

1) U.N. Expert Working Group on Industrial Programming Data, United Nations, New York, 17-19 May 1961, convened by the Division of Industrial Development of the Department of Economic and Social Affairs (predecessor of today's UNIDO).

2) Thomas Vietorisz, "Programming Data Summary for the Chemical Industry", Industrialisation and Productivity Bulletin 10, U.N., New York (1966), pp.7-56.

The same approach has been applied more systematically by Robert Ayres of the International Research and Technology Corporation to the technology choice model for PVC production[1]. Distinguishing five process levels (chlorine production, ethylene production, ethylene dichloride production, vinyl chloride production and polyvinyl chloride production), and identifying altogether 26 different unit processes available for these five levels, he shows that there are 133 alternative process chains for producing VCM, which is followed by three alternative ways of polymerizing. Considering the existing plants in the U.S., however, one finds only 12 process chains leading to VCM (or 36 ways of getting to PVC).

For example, out of the 7 alternative ways of producing chlorine, the actual U.S. practice uses only the process of salt electrolysis (mercury cell and diaphram cell) and the process by brine electrolysis and carboration; neither HCl oxidation (with $CuCl_2$ or HNO_3 as a catalyst) nor the modified solvay process for NH_4Cl oxidation is in use. Ethylene is produced from either propane or ethane, but not from naphtha (light or full range). Dichloethylene is mostly via gas-phase direct chlorination, while the liquid-phase chlorination and oxychlorination of ethylene are not in actual use. VCM from ethylene-dichloride pyrolysis is the most popular, but when VCM is produced from concentrated acetylene or acetylene/ethylene via the Wulff process, the unit processes specified for the preceding three levels are by-passed. The processes to produce VCM from ethylchloride, from ethane oxychlorination, and from ethylene chlorination are not actually used in the U.S. However, the model asserts that continued current use should not be a fool-proof criterion for technology choice; but an optimum process chain ought to be discovered in each case as a cost-minimising solution under given particular economic constraints (factor prices, raw material cost, utility and energy cost, cost imputable to polluting effluent, marketability of by-products, etc.).

Consider technologically less sophisticated fields of industry, such as sugar refinery and shoe production. For example, James Pickett and David J.C. Forsyth report (though still only

---

1)　The model developed by the Corporation with support from the National Science Foundation Contract C-652 (A materials process - product model for the chlorinated plastics industry, 1972).

98733

informally) on their Appropriate Technology Research Project(1),
which attempted to evaluate the technologies used in a few factories operating in Ethiopia and Ghana, in comparison with those
actually employed in British factories with comparable product
lines. The group soon realised that the problem of choice of technology could not be satisfactorily dealt with unless one examined
systematically a much wider spectrum of alternative technologies
than those embodied in the British counterpart. They thus included
manufacturers of capital goods in their data gathering industrial
visits in the United Kingdom, and further decided to go beyond the
three original countries in search of alternative technologies.

The manufacturing of raw sugar from cane can be broken down
into as many as 9 basic processes: weighing and sampling of cane,
milling, clarification, filtration, evaporation, crystalization,
centrifugal separation and drying. Raw sugar resulting from these
processes, is further affinated, melted, clarified, filtrated,
decoloured, crystalised, centrifuged and dried, to obtain refined
sugar. Each of these processes is subject to a few to a dozen
alternative methods of operation: e.g. milling by manual crushing,
by mortar and pestle, by roller mills, by screw crusher, etc; when
power is involved, manual, ox, water, wind, etc., may not be ruled
out; clarification by continuous or batch process, with manual or
automatic liming, sulphitation and/or carbonation; filtration by
bag, by plate and frame filters, or by vacuum filters; boiling by
vacuum pans, either batch or continuous (in the case of the conventional vacuum pan process), by open hot sulphitation pans or
open boiling pans with alternative furnace designs (in the case
of the Indian Khandsari process); etc. Again, in a shoe factory,
producing 1,200 pairs of men's cemented shoes with unit soles per
shift, one would normally see 80 to 90 separate processes and some
50 different machines in operation.

The use of a particular equipment for a particular process
or sub-process may affect the choices available for the rest of
the production line, technically and economically. E.g. the choice
of crushing mill affects the output of bagasse; since bagasse is
used as a boiler fuel, this affects the choice of boiler. Also the
cost of operating two otherwise inferior sub-processes may be cut
substantially if it proves possible to use in one sub-process any
spare labour capacity on the other. Thus a minute examination

---

1) Carried out by the Overseas Development Unit of the University
   of Strathclyde, United Kingdom.

reveals that the number of possible permutations of alternative operations is likely to be very large - so large that a serious model for choice of technology would have to make recourse to a computer programme. The Strathclyde Project was originally intended to demonstrate empirically how the profitability analysis in terms of market prices and shadow prices could work as a tool of appraisal of the appropriateness of technology at the plant level. But it soon became clear that a practical theory of choice of technology could not dispense with the task of creating some special framework of analysis in one form or another that would necessarily be highly information-intensive. This should shed light on the basic question of how to assimilate technological information.

Chapter X

THE ROLE OF "ENGINEERING" IN THE TRANSFER OF TECHNOLOGY

For a considerable number of participants the role of engineering services and the organisations which supply them seemed very important, and seemed also to be in need of research. This preoccupation was reflected in the concluding session discussions[1] and it is now reflected in the Development Centre's programme of activities.

At the same time there was not much detailed discussion of this subject, and there was little attempt to explore in depth the wide divergencies of assumptions made by different participants. There was a very marked divergence between the formal presentation by Judet and Perrin of IREP (supported by a number of working documents)[2], which was perhaps characteristically French, in its approach, and the reactions of some "anglo-saxon" participants. The IREP presentation incorporated fairly radically nationalist assumptions about the location, ownership and control of such engineering activities. Some participants felt that it was philosophically somewhat a priori and schematic. These "anglo-saxons"

---

1) See Part One, Chapter XI and Part Two, I.
2) Background Papers No. 2, 13, 33 and 34.

assigned a much less "ideological" role to consulting and contracting activities, while not on the whole denying their practical importance.

The term "engineering" has several rather different uses in English, and there are additional translation difficulties into French. In their major general discussion of engineering(1) the IREP team distinguish two main usages in English:

  i) a British usage in which "engineering" refers to the industry which produces capital goods - the "function of production";

  ii) an American usage in which "engineering" refers to the elaboration of designs and projects - the "function of conception and realisation".

They argue that in Europe and in France, the term "engineering" has been borrowed from the USA and is used in the American sense. Very recently, a French word, "ingénierie", has been created to correspond to the American sense. However, IREP continues to use the American word(2) since it is currently used in the technical press and in international meetings.

In their now considerable empirical work, covering a number of developed and developing countries, the IREP team have developed a view about the evolution of engineering, which is important to their assessment of the present situation. Aspects of this view were outlined to the Study Group by Perrin(3), and are contained in Background Papers 2, 13, 33 and 34. In the widely circulated UNIDO paper(4), Judet and Perrin say:

> Engineering is an autonomous function of design and construction of industrial installations. (Engineering is also tied to the design and construction of large

_____

1) "L'Engineering (Rapport Provisoire)". Judet, Perrin and Tibergein. IREP. Université des Sciences Sociales de Grenoble, May, 1970.

2) Except in their major study conducted for the French authorities.

3) See, for example, his intervention in Chapter XI and his note in Part Two.

4) The transfer of technology in an integrate programme of industrial development, UNIDO/IPPD.53, Vienna, 15th October, 1971, p.10.

buildings and infrastructure work, but here our paper deals with industrial engineering.) Up to recent times the design and construction function had not acquired autonomy; it was closely tied to the production function from which it was not yet distinguished.

During the last decades, following the size of plants to be constructed, the growing complexity of techniques to be mastered, the design and building of coherent and efficient industrial production units is no longer conceivable for a genial artisan nor a talented constructor. The design and implementation function had to be distinguished from the production function. Its autonomy was confirmed by setting up on the one hand design departments and new projects departments and on the other hand independent consultant groups (consulting engineers) and specialised or diversified engineering firms.

Engineering is characterised by a set of methods and structures which enable a mastery of technical, scientific, technological, economic and financial information necessary for the conversion of capital into a coherent set of productive forces. At a time when the increasing complexity of techniques renders this conversion very difficult, engineering is precisely the agent of this onerous process. It is geared to optimisation: optimisation in terms of delays and costs of parts and sub-units of the industrial plant and optimisation of the running costs of this industrial plant in terms of quality and cost of the product.

There is a further semantic point which may have important implications. The American usage of "engineering", even as a noun, refers to an activity. The IREP team, however, frequently use it to refer to an organisation which performs these activities. So, in their French language texts, IREP authors frequently refer to an "engineering", meaning an agency which carries out design and supervision (of construction) activities. However, this usage does not exist in English language contexts. It seems that the IREP researchers find it convenient to speak of an "engineering" because they think in terms of a central function to which there corresponds a characteristic organisation. On the whole, in English language contexts(1), the usage is more fragmented and there is no single English language term which corresponds to this usage in French.

In different contracts, the "engineering" of a project may be done by: independent firms of consultant engineers, non-independent firms of consultant engineers, the project's promotors, affiliates of the project's promotors, equipment suppliers, process licensors, or a mixture of all these. The IREP researchers do not, of course, completely deny this. They do, however, believe strongly in the importance of a "functional" activity - engineering - which has functional relations with other activities and they believe in organisations which correspond to these functions. One aspect of this is their implied emphasis on the singularity and unity of the function and the corresponding organisation. Coupled with the IREP researchers' relatively radical nationalist views about technological and economy dependency, the clear conclusion is a need for the creation of "national engineerings" in LDCs. Perrin says "The 'engineering' firms of developed countries which are involved in investment projects in less developed countries possess their own logic: to promote the sale of equipment from their country of origin. These firms necessarily tend to develop the turn-key formula for export sales ..... The firms ..... through their involvement in LDCs, accumulate experience and knowledge which is fed back into their own industrial system. There is thus a transfer in the wrong direction. To transfer technologies or rather to master technology, an LDC should create its own engineering firm."(2)

The IREP presentation offers a scheme of four "poles" in an integrated programme of industrial development. These are:

i) production (of final goods);

ii) the supply of capital equipment and plant, which embodies technology;

iii) engineering;

iv) research and development.

Engineering, however, provides a schematic focal point at which the other three poles interact: hence its supreme importance.

1) One might say "Anglo-saxon contexts".
2) Background Paper No.34. Underlining by the Development Centre.

In the IREP view the four poles are increasingly closely linked internationally in a vertical integration, and in particular Judet and Perrin appear to believe that engineering firms must necessarily be linked with particular manufacturers of capital equipment. Judet says: "It is important to stress the part played by the engineering consultancy firms which are subsidiaries, whether recognised as such or not, of multinational firms in order to:

- secure the conversion of the product into a "merchandise" package (role of engineering consultants in building power stations, turn-key plants, etc.);

- ensure the pre-eminence of world technological processes (companies licensed for the major technological processes, which they undertake to use);

- enlarge the distribution channels for the merchandise, co-ordinate them, etc., for the sole benefit of the multinational firms."(1)

Thus the IREP presentation on the role of "engineering" is closely related to its views on multinational firms which are equally radical(2). In the IREP scheme of desirable LDC industrialisation, there seems little possible useful role for manufacturing subsidiaries of foreign firms (who could dispense with the need for an "engineering" intermediary). Almost necessarily, therefore, the transfer of technology must be made through an "engineering".

The IREP researchers lay great stress on the role of information in relation to modern industry. The organisation which provides engineering services has the key role in acquiring and handling the information. Whether or not the international "engineering" is closely linked to process licensors and equipment suppliers - we have seen that the IREP researchers believe that it generally is - the technology user in the developing country suffers a new type of dependency, oriented towards the engineering organisation(3). This reinforces the more traditional causes of economic dependency.

---

1) Background Paper No.2, pp.10, 11.
2) See Chapter III and Background Papers 2 and 33 (summarised in Part Three).
3) See the exchange of views in Chapter XI, notably between Perrin, Sabato and de Bandt.

The IREP emphasis on the central importance of engineering
and its role in promoting technological dependency is based on
their extensive case studies. These include several relatively
mature LDCs (India, Mexico, Turkey) and two Eastern European
countries (Hungary, Roumania)(1). However, the views have been
developed to some extent on the basis of a study of Japan(2) and
on the basis of a major, officially sponsored, survey in France(3).
This French study is based partly on existing documentation in the
technical press and in the files of several official agencies, but
more importantly on a series of interviews with a sample of 40
French engineering organisations. This research (and the Japanese
study) was not directly concerned with LDC problems. However, the
IREP researchers believe that the interrelations between engineering, and the other "poles" in industrial development present similar problems for most developed countries as for LDCs.

IREP has, also, in the context of its consulting services to
the Algerian Ministry of Industry and Energy, begun to turn its
attention to the problems of industrially less mature LDCs(4).
Perrin described briefly some of the conclusions. One conclusion,
based on the experience of the national steel corporation (CNS)(5)
concerns the difficulty of establishing a satisfactory contractual
working basis for using foreign engineering services, in a case
where embryo national engineering and equipment manufacturing
capabilities exist but where these clearly do not have the technical and know-how capacity to be the major agents in a project. The
IREP conclusion is relatively radical: to be prepared to sacrifice

---

1) Engineering en Inde, Roberts and Perrin. November 1970.
   Engineering en Inde, Tome II; Roberts. March, 1972.
   La Société Nationale Mexicaine PEMES et l'engineering,
   La Vega Navarro, December, 1970.
   Engineering en Turquie, Turkkam and Erdemli, March 1971.
   Planification des industries mécaniques et situation de
   L'engineering en Hongrie, Judet and Perrin, November-December,
   1970.
   L'engineering en Roumanie, Perrin, April, 1972.

2) Engineering au Japon, Turkkam, July 1972.

3) Place et fonction de l'ingénièrie dans le système industriel
   français, Perrin, March 1973.

4) Le développement des capacités d'engineering en Algerie.
   Rapport de synthèse. February 1973. This report is confidential.

5) And also on the experience of major public sector steel and
   fertiliser corporations in India.

some administrative efficiency in design and implementation of projects in order to move as soon as possible towards a system doing no more than hiring foreign individuals with appropriate know-how. The IREP researchers are sceptical about the merits of LDC national engineering organisations accepting either a sub-contracting role in relation to a foreign engineering contractor, or even a role of integrated responsibility and joint activities.

A number of points were made by other participants which are relevant to this somewhat radical view of the importance of "engineering". First, it seemed that the IREP is primarily concerned with (technologically) relatively advanced industries in the modern sector. This seems to reflect the belief, that unless a country can have an independent technology and a capacity to implement the more advanced technologies, it is condemned to some sort of general structural technological dependence. This means that great emphasis is placed on developing as wide a range of capital goods industries as possible, and on having the R and D needed to develop these industries physically located in the using country. At the other extreme is a view, argued in parts by some participants, that for most of the industrial activities that LDCs want to establish, there is a range of alternative technologies readily available. They are readily available to some extent because the technology is incorporated in fairly standard, widely used plant and equipment, or because there are a number of competing processes available or because the patents involved have expired. This sort of line was argued in relation to both chemicals (Giral) and metal working (Boon), industries which IREP had offered as examples of relatively extreme technological dependence. Those who take this view do not need to claim that there are no problems about the pricing of the technology transferred.

So the IREP presentation was challenged by those who argued that technology, or a technology, should be thought of rather as a series of products which are traded internationally and whose prices are determined in the (more or less imperfect) market place (Sabato, Giral). This attempt to demythologise the technology transfer process was reinforced by those who argued that there are many different ways in which "technology" is acquired. Some participants (de Bandt, Stepanek) directly challenged the view that "engineering" services are necessarily supplied by organisations which are effectively dominated by process licensors or equipment suppliers. There are many different types of "engineering" service and a large variety of organisations which supply them internationally. A

relatively extreme, almost laisser-faire, view(1), would be that
"import substitution" in this type of product should be treated,
like import substitution for other products, as a matter of comparative advantage: the key question is the availability of the
necessary skills and their opportunity cost when employed in a
particular use.

The question of the costs of establishing national "engineerings" was not discussed in any detail by the participants; if the
problem is posed in the IREP terms, the economic case for establishing such national engineerings is overwhelming, and the only
questions are about the technical feasibility in different national
cases. However, Perrin suggested that a future (perhaps Development
Centre) research project might usefully seek to make a comparative
assessment of the costs of establishing national engineerings versus the costs of association agreements with foreign technology
suppliers.

It seemed to some participants that views such as those developed by the IREP researchers had relatively pessimistic implications
for a large number of small LDCs, particularly in Africa. The IREP
view stresses the dangers of technological dependency, and the
difficulties of breaking it in a world dominated by technology
suppliers. At the same time, it stresses the importance of modern
industries and technologies. Most important, the IREP exponents
are not at all naive about the possibilities for international or
national information services. Such services may have an important
role to play, but they cannot act as substitutes for efficient
engineering organisations. IREP researchers stress the proprietary
value of much vital technical information and the importance of
know-how. However, the IREP researchers have so far concentrated
mainly on relatively industrialised "mature" LDCs - India, Morocco,
Turkey. Moreover, Algeria, one might argue, is a rather special
case, for which the attractive raw material base, geographical
location and population size make rapid industrialisation an attractive possibility. The IREP group have not yet considered in
depth what one might say about the "engineering" problems, possibilities and requirements of less favoured LDCs. For some participants this problem was less acute, in that they did not share the
IREP emphasis on technologically relatively advanced industries.

Some participants also felt that concern about organisational
and political aspects of the role of engineering services tends to

---

1) This view would not be far from that attributed by some to
    some earlier Development Centre publications.

obscure more basic (and more properly technological) issues. To
the extent that technologies can be "unpacked" - in technologists'
sense - into particular process alternatives (as discussed in
Chapter IX), one becomes interested in the capacity of different
types of engineering organisation to exploit the resulting possibilities to obtain and implement the most appropriate technologies
for particular situations. Some participants felt that questions
of the nationality, ownership and organisation of engineering
activities can be overemphasised, to the detriment of consideration
of technical capacity and technological independence. In many situations, the important aspects are the technical competence and
experience of the engineering organisations, its capacity to acquire
and manipulate technological information and its ability to gain
access to alternative privileged sources. Central national engineering organisations of the type advocated by UNIDO (and IREP) are
not necessarily better placed from this point of view than established international, engineering service organisations: the problem then becomes one of a trade-off of different kinds of advantage
and comparatively little attention has been paid to the more narrowly "technological" capabilities of engineering service organisations in relation to the requirements of LDCs. The Development
Centre is considering undertaking research in this difficult, but
apparently basic, area: it would focus initially on the technological capabilities and adaptability of the conventional international
engineering consulting organisations.

Chapter XI

INDUSTRIAL AND TECHNOLOGICAL INFORMATION SERVICES

As a subject for discussion, the term "information" often
exerts a magical effect. It serves as a cross-road where different
issues connect themselves and different professions find themselves
almost equally qualified to take part. The November meeting turned
out to be no exception in this respect. On the contrary, the merit
of the discussion actually held on the subject seems to lie in its
very "participatory" nature. It pointed to the diversity of factors

and actors involved in the complex mechanism whereby industrial and technological information is generated, transformed and assimilated for various levels and kinds of decision problems: a feature which would not have emerged had the same subject been debated within the circle of information service specialists alone.

The discussion threw up a number of difficult issues which were discussed before. First, perhaps a majority of participants were close to arguing that - at least for the benefit of LDCs - private ownership of intellectual property should be abolished. LDCs should have free access to information at present covered by licences and patents. Some participants were also arguing for a much more forward move by LDC government agencies into the grey area of knowledge not legally protected under licence and patent law but jealously guarded by its present owners. Others felt that this concern was somewhat naive, and that LDC governments could not gain usable access to particular processes and know-how simply by the legal act of abolishing (or severely limiting) intellectual private property or by establishing a national technology agency.

A second related issue is the extent to which information requirements and possibilities may vary from one use situation to another. There are a spectrum of use situations and requirements. One very difficult one concerns the technology information requirements for process choice and design at the plant level. Can an international (or national) information service have a credible role here in supplying the information required by the technology importer? Another extreme could be detailed commercial market information about a product. The problem is to decide how far to treat these as extreme cases and to go ahead with establishing international information services on the assumption that most cases can be adequately covered by such services.

On the whole the discussion contributed very little to the technical problems related to the planning and management of any particular technical information centres. But the proceedings clearly indicate that the recent rapid progress in information technology has led to the evolution of a specialised profession, whose achievements in turn have prompted our perception of the vast grey area concerning questions of real substance and channels of information, which cannot be affected by that profession alone. In order to do justice to the particularly animated discussion which consumed a good three hours, an almost verbatim transcript is reproduced here. This may also serve the purpose of conveying the general atmosphere of the three-day meeting which has been substantially disregarded in the writing of the preceding Chapters.

VERBATIM PROCEEDINGS

M. Daya:

I think the real problem is that of access to scientific and technical information at present held by multinational firms. The Maghreb Centre of Industrial Studies constantly runs up against the lack of efficient networks of information. The three member countries have reached a certain level of industrial development and business managers are not "illiterates". They most strongly desire access to technical information for pre-investment studies of new industrial projects. For example, we have been asked for information on the production of aluminium fluoride from fluor spar. We have approached several national and international organisations, but have only been able to get very fragmentary information on companies in Switzerland and Italy which hold such a process, which it should be added, they were ready to sell to us. We have been unable to obtain any information on French, British and American processes. How can one make a choice under these circumstances? We therefore often ask if it is possible to establish an international organisation to acquire processes for resale to developing member countries. At least it could serve as a more practical and efficient link between suppliers and customers for technological processes.

G. Dardenne:

My organisation (the Association for the Promotion of Agro-industry - APRIA) is concerned with information in the food and agriculture industries. I think that there are ways for developing countries to gain access to many of the so-called secrets, and that companies in developed countries are quite open to furnishing "know-how" under reasonable financial arrangements, on which the parties can agree between themselves. I join Mr. Daya in asking why OECD does not play the role of intermediary between developing countries and the firms in developed countries which have "know-how".

D. Carrière:

In my work in Algeria in connection with S.N. Metal, I was struck by the lack of information on ironworks. This information in fact exists, but among the iron-masters in developed countries. "Chemical Abstracts" has been able to reconstruct products by cross-checking fragmentary information fed into a computer. Equipment can

be reconstituted from information in manufacturers' prospectuses.
At present, there is a tightening of information in the specialised
organs of the metal industry.

However, the existing information network is a network of the
rich; information must be paid for. The basic question is how to
develop a better communication network between developed and
developing countries. I would like to suggest that the Development
Centre should study the curbs, the obstacles to this communication.
The superabundance of information and the secrecy which exists in
developed countries inevitably lead to industrial spying. Industrial
espionage is the result of a lack of communication.

In the course of these discussions, technology has appeared
to be inseparable from the market, but it was also pointed out that
multinational firms prefabricate the demand. The channels should
not be confused with the content of the transfer. Developing countries are mature and quite capable of making their own technological
adaptations. They look for progress solely in the possibilities of
choice offered by the wealthy nations. I propose that UNIDO and the
OECD Development Centre should study "communicability" at the planning and the enterprise level, and should pinpoint the precise
problem to be tackled identifying the elements which block this
communication.

J. Giral Barnes

We all know that equipment sellers give very detailed information on equipment, which cannot be handled by the concept of a
general clearing house. There are thousands of industrial associations and a huge quantity of pamphlets of firms which can give
information on a branch-by-branch basis. To give an example, in
chemical industries there are more than 100,000 processes and
millions of pieces of technical information. When an entrepreneur
decides to build a factory he is supposed to know where to apply
to obtain the appropriate technical information and know-how.

We should distinguish between those simple, small firms which
are technically illiterate, and those big firms which have their
own technologists; their situation from the standpoint of technological information is very different. By "illiterate" I mean those
who do not read scientific and technical journals where many processes are described. I think there was a general consensus as to
the fact that we all could benefit from more information. But this
is where the consensus ended. Therefore, rather than trying to
interpret the feelings of the majority, I will try to give my own

version: we need to analyse the problem better. Call it epistemology, morphological analysis or plain common sense. We have to identify the problem like this:

- What are the needs?

- Who are the end-users? How technically illiterate are they?

- What do they want? (An idea, a pre-investment study, a process selection study, a project, a project optimisation, a technical detail, or the whole thing, lock stock and barrel?)

- What does each country need (by sector, region, etc.)?

- What are the disciplines involved (by subject, pieces of information, types of package, etc.)?

- Who has these disciplines and who needs them?

- How can it be transferred (in terms of channels, costs and prices)?

Once this is done, we can then begin to address ourselves to the following questions:

- What should be the approaches? Are there any methodologies that proved successful somewhere and could be applied to other problems?

- Are there any common denominators in technical skills that merit suggesting a training programme, either at university level or as independent programme or any other way?

- Are there common information needs not covered by the existing information systems that would justify creation of new systems?

J. Perrin:

In dealing with the function of "engineering", we have emphasised the important role played by information. If scientific and technical information, and more generally, scientific and technical knowledge, are regarded as productive forces, this explains the autonomy of engineering. More generally, information is characteristic of the second industrial revolution; the law of the transformation of energy sustained the first industrial revolution; the second is tied to the appearance of machines designed to transform not energy but information. Modern industry, characterised first by mechanisation and later by automation, demands substantial knowledge especially at the stage of plant design and engineering - more than at the production stage. Industrial branches are affected differently by this development. It is more significant in continuous processing industries: chemicals, petrochemicals, cement, etc. In these industries the production stage becomes less important than that of design and construction (but also maintenance). It is in this kind of context that we must approach the question of transfer of technology or rather the command of technologies. And the problems of effecting such transfers necessarily reflect the importance and the strategic role of information, and scientific and technical knowledge.

For developing countries a new form of dependence is induced by the fact that technical information and know-how is held by private engineering firms. These firms accumulate data and exchange it with Third World countries, but their own position is strengthened by the application of their techniques in new surroundings. The resulting transfer of knowledge is in the wrong direction. Two measures can therefore be proposed to overcome this situation:

i) the creation of national engineering firms in developing countries, and

ii) the creation of technological information services within international organisations such as UNIDO.

Such information services would deal particularly with the diffusion of information on:

- different processes for principal products;
- holders of these "processes" and engineering firms specialised in them;
- data related to principal "processes" : inputs, by-products, minimum break-even points possibilities of miniaturisation, identification of scarce factors, implied costs, approximate breakdown of capital goods needed to carry out these processes.

J. Sabato:

The previous speaker just mentioned the question of engineering consulting firms. I should like to point out that the role of these firms is to sell knowledge considered as a commodity. These firms penetrate everywhere and I wonder how a national engineering consultant group proposed by Mr. Perrin could get the technology. This technological information has to be purchased from these firms.

J. de Bandt:

Would it not be wise to distinguish between technical know-how geared to production and the "commercial" aspect of engineering? I believe that engineering firms must be very specialised. Manufacturers also play an important role in the diffusion of technology. To study the role of consultant engineers and manufacturers, we must look at the technological information system as a whole. Finally, I wish to emphasise that little technical information is essential, economic information is equally important.

J.P. Fernandez:

I hear many people say that developed countries should make information available for less-developed countries and that UNIDO could play a big role in this field. But this does not mean that it would be possible to establish a data bank to give information on all technical processes. International organisations cannot be technology brokers: these brokers exist in the private sector, and they cost money.

Every developing country should establish a technical information service (like ours) to provide local entrepreneurs with the appropriate technical information. Advice and funds may be obtained through multilateral and bilateral aid sources. These local services would be responsible for locating information, first locally, and then, if little (or no) information is found, from international organisations as well as information centres which exist in developed countries. A considerable part of this information may be obtained without charge or for a small fee. However, know-how and more detailed information is not easily accessible and its cost is high.

G. Boon:

I believe that there is a need for a specialised machinery that could let us know whether all the technological alternatives have been considered, in each practical case. An exchange centre for demand and supply of technological information, with the participation of firms both from developing and developed countries could allow the current situation to be overcome. Such an agency should list and classify the adaptation possibilities in the technological field.

T. Fox:

VITA is very much interested in the setting up of an international information service on technology, in co-operation with other organisations. The current information services, many of which are located outside the LDCs have to be reinforced and their information should be constantly updated. But there are a few basic questions one should not neglect in talking of an international information service. VITA received nearly 2,500 requests last year. Of these, some 35 per cent came through the OECD Development Enquiry Service; some 50 per cent came from overseas, AID Technicians, etc. Our major problem is the distance separating requestors from respondents. I do not believe we have succeeded in building a system that is truly sensitive to real local needs; real users of our information are located in many remote corners of the world who actually do not speak to us. Another problem relates to the difficulty of obtaining fresh information. Outdated information is easy to acquire but useless. The real sources of information, too, are located far away.

G.G. Schweitzer:

I wish to cite one example of successful information transfer. In early 1970 an experimental project was undertaken by AID in collaboration with NASA to determine to what extent certain types of technology developed under NASA auspices and stored in the NASA technology data bank could be adapted and transferred to developing countries. The Korea Institute of Science and Technology (KIST) and the Illinois Institute of Technology have been selected as the transfer agents. Several "hard transfers" to Korean commercial manufacturers are now in various stages of completion: miniature transceivers, high sensitivity communications circuits, all-purpose survival rations, food packaging, etc. The cost of this project was US$150,000, but it has already generated US$100,000 worth of KIST contract work for the Korean Government and industry. The experiment is considered to have been successful, both in clarifying many aspects of the technology transfer process and in upgrading Korean technological capabilities.

M. Usui:

I believe that the points raised by Mr. Fox regarding the real sources and the real users of information are well taken. In May, 1971, an international professional group was organised under the

auspice of certain French Government agencies to examine a broad
range of problems facing the various kinds of data bank for
developmental planning and policy purposes(1). The Group examined
the "diseases of data banks" at three levels: data sources,
decision models for development, and users of data banks. The
proceedings of the meeting have a sub-title: "Puisque ces mystères
nous dépassent, feignons d'en être l'organisateur" (Molière).
Indeed many of the diseases eroding the existing and the newly
evolving data bank projects appear to be the more obvious, the
larger is the community of users to be covered and the greater
is the diversity of needs and decision problems to be catered for.
I am afraid that the diseases can get far more serious with the
information service projects handled by international bureaucracies.
I am not at all sure if this basic practical question has been
studied adequately before so many expert groups have agreed in
recommending the building of so many new information centres for
the benefit of developing countries.

The weakest part of most information service projects seems
to relate to their capability to comprehend the very decision
problems for which they are supposed to provide information. When
we come to questions of technological information for industry,
it is not enough just to have a scientific and technological
information centre; such a centre may function well for scientists
and R and D specialists; if properly digested and integrated, the
existing scientific and technological documents could satisfy a
great part of the information needs. Who is doing such a job? And
for whom? You will note that the information needs are expressed
in fact more frequently by those who do not understand technology
in technologists' terms. Is the existing convention of indexing
technological information by the so-called document handling
specialists adequate to respond to the needs of industrialists?
Also, are not such concepts as "model plants", "minimum economical
plant sizes", etc. basically misleading when we are concerned about
broadening scope for the LDC choice of technology? When I was with
UNIDO, I produced those "Profiles of Manufacturing Establishments",
but the real theme of this series seems to have been often mis-
understood. The real theme was to show how industrial establishments differ from one another by the time they have become

---

1) Data Banks for Development : Proceedings of the International
Expert Meeting, Saint-Maximin, 24-28 May, 1971. Observatoire
Economique Méditerranéen/INSEE Marseille, Paris, La Documenta-
tion Francaise, 1972, XVII - 242 p.

economically viable units. The theme is only half-baked, because there is a basic classification problem yet to be settled for industrial technology. I wonder if Mr. Giral's concept of "technology modules", and/or the concept of "process analysis" in industrial economics, should receive more serious attention from the standpoint of the information specialist's classification problem as well.

As regards Mr. Schweitzer's appraisal of the experience of KIST, I have no doubt that the project was a success in one respect. When I visited the Republic of Korea I encountered a number of Korean industrialists who did not seem to feel very happy about the success of that project. The point was perhaps that KIST could immediately affect the technology of only a handful of relatively privileged customers. Indeed, its possible spill-over and spin-off effects that affect the Korean industrial society more broadly can occur only very slowly. But to facilitate this process, there is a question of strategy as to how to foster indigenous engineering consulting firms; how the numerous government-fed quasi-business research institutes can develop a closer link with industry; how those industrialists in the intermediate and lower classes who have in fact contributed so much to the spectacular growth of Korean industry in the past years, can be made to understand that information does not have to be embodied in equipment but should be searched and paid for as a commodity of commerce.

M. Seki:

Many international organisations are running, or wish to run, information services specialised in technological questions. There is also a proposal to set up an international centre to be run under the direction of several LDC governments. I wish to see more clearly how all these proposals as a whole are likely to evolve into a better network of communication among developing countries and between advanced and developing countries. The particular problem that arouses my interest is also how to digest the huge amount of information available in developed countries and how to adapt this information to the needs of developing countries. The point made by Mr. Usui on modules and channels seems to me to be very important and I strongly recommend to the Development Centre as well as to my own organisation, APO, that it be studied in further depth.

S. Teitel:

I, too, would like to stress the importance of the methodological points made by Mr. Usui. "Technological information for
whom" is indeed the question that ought to receive a more methodical treatment. Technological information for national planning
offices, pre-investment industrial studies, etc. is not exactly
the same thing as technological information for process designers,
industrial researchers, etc. But the former requires a substantial
degree of pre-digestion of the latter. Also questions of secrecy,
obstacles, high costs of technology have been raised without
clearly defining information "on what" and "for whom". If one
starts defining it really carefully, perhaps one finds that there
is no short-cut in dealing with the information problem in its
entirety. Nothing can circumvent the need for the basic infrastructure, educational, scientific and technical services, information consultancy and other industry-related services.

J. de Bandt:

That means, I think, that we must distinguish between general
information on processes and practical information on the manufacture of a given machine. In the same way there must be a distinction between information sold as a self-contained commodity
and information incorporated in the equipment to be sold. With
regard to Mr. Usui's proposals on the definition of a model of
technological information and on the standardisation of classification systems, I think that the former is valid, but that the
latter is foredoomed. Classification systems differ because they
correspond to different kinds of information.

J. Torcol:

Apart from information service proper, one should not neglect
the need for an improved mechanism of communication among the
existing research institutes. In my Institute (Institut pour la
Technologie et l'Industrialisation des Produits Agricoles Tropicaux,
Abijan), we would conduct a survey of the work being undertaken in
various research institutes in the field of food industry, and
organise meetings among them in order to improve the reciprocal
information flow and to avoid duplicating research efforts.

K.L. Nanjappa:

In India, we have developed an information service, which
covers technological, management and economic guidance to small-

scale entrepreneurs. The services have been evolved to suit the
indigenous systems and requirements of individuals. We have a chain
of institutes and extension centres which are equipped with laboratories and workshops. These are manned by qualified and experienced
persons with specialisation in selected fields. This organisation
has worked well in providing extension and consultancy services to
entrepreneurs, as suited to local requirements. The entrepreneurs
are guided on various aspects of industry, including prospective
areas of investment, choice of product, product-mix, product design,
raw materials, processes, machinery, factory lay out, sources of
availability of finance, potential markets and profitability. Individual counselling is provided by post and personally to the visit-
ing entrepreneurs at the Institutes. Testing and demonstration
facilities for processes are offered through workshops and laboratories. This is supplemented by factory visits by Institute personnel to the individuals and on-the-spot guidance and assistance in
solving problems.

Besides these extensive operations, we carry out intensive
assistance, through in-plant studies. A team of technical and
management experts stay on in an individual factory, study the
entire operating system, analyse it and prepare a report which
locates the weaknesses to be made up in order to attain higher
profitability, efficiency, cost reduction and streamlining the
whole set up.

We have brought out a considerable volume of literature which
includes information on governmental assistance, procedural formali-
ties, prospective industries in selected areas, model schemes or
project outlines, product-studies, feasibility studies indicating
the size of production, investment and profitability, area studies,
pamphlets – Towards Better Techniques – which suggest improved and
efficient systems both for technological and management aspects,
blue-prints and product designs. Open-house discussions are organised in collaboration with experts, academicians, businessmen,
technologists and the specific group of local small entrepreneurs
under the aegis of the Institutes, where they discuss and thrash
out general as well as individual problems. The basic ingredient
of the programme is adaptation and development of indigenous systems to suit local requirement.

Foreign collaboration with individual small-scale firms is
also allowed, but this programme has worked on a very limited
scale. Larger international co-operation in this field would help
mutually for while we have primarily capital-saving, labour-

intensive systems, we are open to adapt the latest technology in
a few selected lines, and can change over from our traditional
(labour-intensive) approach.

Recognising the role of ancillary industries, we have recently
set up two sub-contracting exchanges with UN assistance. These act
as clearing houses for information regarding the requirements of
large producers and the production capacity available with the
small firms. These centres also provide technological assistance
to small entrepreneurs.

A documentation centre for collection and transmission of
suitable and latest technological information available abroad to
local entrepreneurs has also been contemplated and international
co-operation in this regard would be welcome. We can also share
our experience with those developing countries whose requirements
will suit our system.

P.C. Trussel:

I heartily subscribe to Mr. Sabato's statement that R and D,
technical information and know-how are all marketable commodities.
Our concern is to see that developing countries get a fair deal on
anything they pay for.

M. Ikonikoff:

With a view to mitigating the adverse effects of the present
technology transfer system, the idea has been mooted of organising
new forms of transfer on an international scale, outside the control of private firms. A number of proposals have been made on the
organisation of the exchange and of dissemination of technical
information so that it can be made available to countries capable
of using it, without their being subject to the restraints involved
in private contracts for technology transfer. It is in this context
that the creation of a technical data bank sponsored by international organisations has been proposed. It would, however, be
naive to pretend to create an international centre capable of
supplying technical information to developing countries. The most
realistic course is to sign agreements with the holders of this
information.

P. Gonod:

In the information field, we have found that in every country
of Latin America there is a lack of information on technological

alternatives that exist in other countries of the region. The eleven principal countries of Latin America participated in our pilot project of the Organisation of American States (OAS). This project has implications in the matter of scientific and technological information:

i) One of its aims is to identify information on technological alternatives;

ii) Identification of specific information needs through the creation of national focal points and by taking an inventory of the information available on existing technologies in each country;

iii) Contacts will be made with the USA, Canada, Japan and the Socialist countries to collect information on a world-wide scale;

iv) The fourth phase will be that of the evaluation of technological information;

v) The last stage will be the selection by each enterprise of the most suitable technology.

Some attempts have been made at the international level to select technology. There seem to exist certain factors limiting such efforts. There have been many pilot projects for which little "follow-up" action has taken place. It would be essential for the success of our pilot project that the compilation of information "unpacked" technologies available at various places be undertaken on a world-wide scale.

P. de Lorenzi:

I recall that the Conferences held under the aegis of OAS in Punta del Este (1967) and Vina del Mar (1969) were not very successful in stimulating the process of technology transfer among the American countries. However, the CACTAL Conference in Brasilia in May 1972 appeared to be quite active on the subject. The conclusions reached by this Conference address the questions concerning information services and information mechanisms; emphasis was put on co-ordination both on a national and on an inter-American basis of the work geared to the improvement of information mechanisms, including those for collecting and evaluating the information necessary to formulate the science and technology policy of the Latin American countries.

J. L. Kahn:

I would like to inform you that the NATR (National Association of Technical Research) has been operating for some time a technological information service which is in a position to reply to the questions of developing countries.

D. Goulet:

Several members of this group evoked the larger ambitions of underdeveloped countries. It is not enough for them to buy patents, obtain licenses or even receive the advice of consultants on a commercial basis. But the crucial question seems to be how to devise appropriate channels through which access to a pool of scientific and technological knowledge can be assured to underdeveloped countries, on other than commercial terms. An overall strategy must begin by pressuring the international economic order in the direction of eventually creating a world-wide technological pool. The aim here, ultimately, is to remove scientific and technological information and arts from the commercial sector.

M. Gérard:

In dealing with the African housing problem, I have made two fundamental observations:

i) The transmission of the data must be in terms of the economy of the developing country in order to avoid any form of "mental colonisation"; and

ii) Engineering plays a large role in the transfer of technological information, but this role also leads to "mental colonisation" since engineering firms are not highly specialised in African matters.

It is therefore necessary for a local engineering profession to be created; developed countries should be invited to aid the developing countries in that matter and to make an effort to translate their techniques into ones that match the economic conditions of the developing countries. In concrete terms, that will mean the construction of documentation networks in order to locate the research, studies, specialised articles, and other information materials possessed by the technical communities of developing countries, and at the same time to sensitise the technical circles in developed countries to other techniques and needs and to assist the developing countries in technical training and in evaluation and verification of technical skills.

R. Colin:

I think that well-managed international co-operation should make it possible to bring into being one or more appropriate technology data banks. This is in line with several aspects of the work of UNIDO, even though this organisation has not brought about the substantial progress which seems possible. In fact, while it is relatively easy to master the problem of collecting and processing technological data, it seems on the other hand that we are far from having a satisfactory system of analysis to handle the reception end and the local environment, or the necessary process of training.

M.A.M. Shabaan:

The issue of overpricing of equipment and technological information cannot be settled without reference to the lack of knowledge of the contractors from developing countries. In Egypt, we have used low cost waste pulp to produce writing paper. This is an example of why developing countries must not completely rely on external sources for complete information about know-how or technology.

A. Latham-Koenig:

There are two basic problems of communication to be tackled: one concerned with the assembly and proper mobilisation of knowledge about appropriate, "intermediate" technologies, the other concerned with its reception and utilisation at the receiving end, in the rural areas of the poor countries. Neither of these "communication systems" currently exist on any significant scale, and their absence constitutes a major gap in the aid and development efforts of both donor and recipient countries. Detailed information about appropriate technologies should be collected, subjected to field trials, and documented in suitable forms for communication to the developing countries. To help solve this difficult question, ITDG is preparing a series of industrial profiles starting with metal and woodworking to provide a range of technologies at varying levels of cost and sophistication. This is being done in collaboration with universities, technical colleges, industrial research organisations and private firms.

N. de Figueiredo:

A high degree of centralisation of information services could be useful in relation to data of a general character: e.g. industry

profiles for programming. But it would not be possible to establish
an information service which gives technical data at the plant
level on a multilateral basis. This is basically a national objective, which can be applied either in a centralised or in a decentralised basis (for big countries such as Brazil and India).
Referring to Mr. Schweitzer's remark on the Republic of Korea, I
should like to add here a note that some of the technological components from the NASA data bank have also been applied successfully
in Brazil: e.g. remote sensing for the survey of natural resources
in the Amazon region.

J. Stepanek:

Neither UNIDO nor the Development Centre could purchase
licenses. International organisations cannot be technology brokers.
What UNIDO is trying to do is to improve the bargaining terms of
developing countries by providing them with proper information.
The publication of the Guidelines for licensing will be very helpful for developing countries in this context.

As the last speaker on this subject, I should like to re-stress
that over the past years the value of consulting companies has been
underestimated whereas the importance of research has been overestimated. It is more important to think of the extension of research
than to make more research which is not put to use. It must be noted
that consulting work is a capital-saving type of activity, whereas
industrial research is a capital-using type of activity. Still
another point that has caught my attention particularly relates to
the distinction between information publicly available and proprietary information. While considerable concern exists about the high
cost of proprietary information and the difficulty in negotiating
for privately held technologies, there is also a realisation that
public information is being inadequately utilised. There are a
number of examples one can cite of new technologies developed
through access to public information alone.

P.M. Henry:

Drawing the lessons from the discussion on the subject of
information, I would recall that the fundamental task of the
Development Centre is that of communication between the developed
and the developing countries. The word "communication" obviously
covers all kinds of particular problems, including information,
terminology, etc. It is evident that there are major regional

differences in the matter of information. Latin America and Asia, the latter in particular, thanks to the Asian Productivity Organisation, have made enormous progress. But in the realm of industrial development, information has generally not made its mark on Africa. The questions raised in the discussions, therefore, have not always concerned the <u>same level of technical information</u>.

Part Two

<u>RAPPORTEURS' SUMMING-UP AND WRITTEN SUBMISSIONS</u>
<u>REVIEWING OR SUPPLEMENTING THE DISCUSSION</u>

INTRODUCTION

The Development Centre Secretariat asked some participants, at the beginning of the Study Group, to act as rapporteurs, that is to sum-up the discussion by highlighting issues which in their view were particularly important and interesting. It was thought, that having several rapporteurs, rather than one, would make the summary more interesting without too much risk of unnecessary repetition; the participants were of several different disciplines and from different corners of the world. This would also permit a more fair representation of the different views. Section I is an edited transcript of the rapporteurs' speeches.

At the close of the proceedings, participants were invited to submit in writing very short statements of their conclusions or impressions. Those that were submitted are reproduced in Section II.

I. RAPPORTEURS' SUMMING-UP

1. F. Stewart

What I want to say is concerned not with what I think the conclusions of the meeting were, but rather with some of the interesting differences that emerged. That, in my view, throws a more interesting pointer to future research requirements than the non-disputed issues do.

There was an important point made about terms earlier on in this session - that terminology is not neutral. The argument was that the strategy which one follows and the terminology which one adopts are related and that therefore terminology is important since it influences our action. I shall mention a few of the terms which were put forward, and the ways in which they influence our action will be immediately obvious. For example, transfer of technology, as someone has pointed out, is not the same as commercialisation; appropriate technology is obviously the right technology;

- 113 -

advanced technology is surely also the best; as is optimum technology; factor price distortions must be a bad thing, and so on.

The influence of terminology on action was brought out in a
particularly interesting manner by Mr. Giral in his discussion of
chemical technology when he pointed out that even in what seem to
be very technical terms, the choice of terminology influences the
ways in which one can look at the problems. Hence, I think we must
be very aware of the fact that our terminology is not value-free
but influences our action and our strategy.

There was some confusion, in the meeting, between technology
transfer and technology generation and adaptation. These are separate issues and it might have been better if we had kept them separate. "Technology transfer" raises interesting problems of price and
also of information channels. "Technology generation and adaptation"
raises various questions about the ways in which one wants to change
the technology and about the ways in which one can go about securing
the change. Technology transfer and technology generation can be
in conflict. Things which make technology transfer easier can indeed make technology generation more difficult. If very sophisticated technology is transferred at a very low price this inhibits
the development of a local technology, and that is another reason
why it is a mistake to confuse these two separate issues. I also
think there is a distinction, which was perhaps blurred over,
between making the appropriate choice of technology in Mr. Stepanek's
terms and choosing the appropriate technology. Making the appropriate choice of technology implies making the best choice among
a given lot of alternatives as does the use of the term optimum
choice of technology. I think, however, that we are interested in
a much broader question, not which is the best choice given the
alternatives today, but in which direction should we change the
choices. How should we generate technology in such a way that we
have a better lot of choices tomorrow? I therefore would like to
see the term 'optimum' eliminated from any discussions of this
subject because it does imply the best and what we are talking
about is really very much the second best - which is the better
among a set of alternatives. We are not talking about the best.
We do not know what the best is - we only know the sort of directions in which we might want to go.

Some interesting differences, which came out quite clearly
on the first day, arose concerning the total diagnosis of the
problem. It seems to me that one could distinguish groups of people

who fall to a lesser or greater extent into different categories(1). There are those who believe that current knowledge about technology is basically satisfactory. In their view, in so far as there is a problem, it is either one of prices or of channels of information. The problem is not one of doing any new work on technology but rather of either getting prices and/or channels of information right.

A second set of people, who also seem to believe that there is no technology problem as such, believe that it is much more a "total structure of society" problem and that if you get the total structure of society right then the technology will automatically adapt itself. I think that it is these people who point to the examples of China and sometimes Tanzania, and who say "get the structure right and you will not have an employment problem, and nor will you have a technology problem, since they are superficial symptoms of what is really not a technology problem at all but a social problem and a problem of world structure". Thus the second group, like the first, but from a very different point of view, does not think that there is a technology problem.

A third group of people do think that there is a technology problem and they think that it is simply a question of getting the same people who used to be working on how to get a man to the moon to work on the right technology. Just as it was quite possible to say that in ten years time we will have a man on the moon, we can say: get the same people, set them on how to get the right technology and in ten years' time we will have solved that problem. I think that this was the sort of philosophy used by some of the aid givers represented here.

Finally, there is a sort of intermediate view held by those who do think that new technology is needed, but recognise that it is also connected with the social structure and therefore would take an intermediate position between the structuralists and the technologists.

Another set of differences which came out on the first day was in the assessment of the contribution of the multinational corporations to the transfer of technology. This is really a factual question, on which more research is needed. There were some who said that, in fact, the multinational corporation contributes

1) Stepanek comments as follows on these three paragraphs: "The category a person finds himself in may vary as that individual views specific technologies. In other words there is more variability in points than has been indicated."

very little and I think Mr. Judet said that this must be so by the very nature of its structure; others, I think Mr. Boon in particular, argued that it did make some contribution. Mr. Schweitzer, who had looked at some of the facts in this connection, said that he had assessed the current contribution as very small. This is therefore a subject on which more empirical research could usually be undertaken.

One general conclusion from the discussions was that of the divorce between technologists, i.e. scientists and engineers, on the one hand, and the users of technology on the other, including economists, who seem to be considered as users rather than as anything else. It was generally felt that there was not very much communication between these two groups of people. I also think that there was a very definite model, in people's minds, of the relationship, between users and technologists and between economists and technologists. Some people seemed to think that the technologists were masters and the economists simply did what they were told within the technological constraints. Others that it was the economists and the users who laid down the specifications and the technologists simply did what they were told within the economic constraints. I do not think either of these models is a realistic one. I believe that both groups of people operate within and in the light of the constraints set by the other, and that there is some sort of circular causation. I therefore think that one could have a much more interesting model of the relationships between users and economists and engineers and scientists. Whatever you think about this relationship, it was very clear that there is a need for much more use of the results of technology and technological research. We heard particularly about food, and to some extent about housing, of ideas that had been discovered but had not in fact been put into use.

This leads to a general point about information services. There was much discussion of such services, but what perhaps was not put clearly enough is that information services are essentially passive(1). Someone did mention that they only respond to people's enquiries. They do not, except in the small scale industry service, go out in the field and propagand for their services, which would be required if one wanted to spread the use of new technology.

Another general point which emerged was the question of whose

_____

1) <u>Professor de Bandt</u> has pointed out that this conclusion does not reflect any consensus in the discussion. He himself doubts its validity.

technology we are talking about. Whom is the technology benefiting?
This depends on the nature of the product which is being investi-
gated which emerged clearly in the discussion of housing. Whose
housing are we promoting? Also in food. Are we looking at low cost
food, are we looking at the current market for products or are we
trying to change the income distribution in the very process of
technology development?

From the interesting discussion and from people's reports
from their technology institutes, it became clear that some work
is being done on what we might call "appropriate technology", that
ideas are being generated, even the multinational corporations are
generating some ideas, and that more ideas will be generated as
more money is put into the field and people report on current
research programmes. But there seemed to be little idea of the
magnitude of the problem, the dimensions of the problem against
which this effort must be assessed and against which, I think,
current effort must be regarded as puny.

Apart from the current magnitude of the problem, of which we
at least can get an idea, if we look at the employment around us,
there seemed to be little idea of the dynamism of the problem.
The fact is that all the time while research institutes working
on appropriate technologies are generating one or two ideas, far
more resources are being put into research in inappropriate technologies in the developed countries. The producers of machinery
in the developed countries persistently continue to expand production of increasingly inappropriate technology for LDCs. We do not
live in a static world; each year technology becomes more capital
intensive and more sophisticated and the gap gets wider between
the needs of the developing countries and what is being provided
by the developed countries. It is against this sort of widening
gap approach that one has to assess current efforts. Some work, the
OECD Development Centre might do in this field, could usefully be
directed at measuring the magnitude of the effort needed and of
the effort actually being made, and the relationship between these
two.

One final point, which was brought up very forcibly by one
of the last speakers yesterday, is that in order to eliminate
technological dependence and to bring about a genuinely appropriate
technology, the technology must essentially come from the country
in which it is used. Although there of course will be trade in
technology, this seems to me an essential criterion for acquiring
an appropriate technology and for eliminating dependence. For that

reason I was sorry that more attention wasn't deovted to this particular problem, and that there weren't more representatives of the developing countries here. I think that some of the philosophy, for example the man on the moon philosophy which I outlined earlier, would lead to continued dependence. If the developed countries are now going to turn their energies to creating what they consider to be an appropriate technology for developing countries the kind of dependence generated in the past will continue, only in a new form(1).

2. B. Behari

I shall not summarise the proceedings but I wish to point to some of the constructive impressions which I myself and, along with me, some other participants might study. Probably it is already well known that the concept of appropriate technology is very confusing and very elusive. One contribution of this study group has been to concretise this concept to some extent. In this context, I would like to recall what Mrs. Stewart said: that appropriate technology does not only include capital equipment needed for industrial production. Indeed it comprises three important aspects, which in my words could be termed as: product design, production process and managerial efficiency. At the same time, you will also recall that Mr. Stepanek said that if we want to transport one technology into another climatic condition, it is possible provided we have the glass house conditions, which means that if the conditions are transported with it then you can produce anything in any other place. But this does not make it an appropriate technology.

I understood that appropriate technology would have to be considered in the local context. If the process of production, the product design, and the managerial efficiency, taken together fit into the particular circumstances, i.e. the particular social,

---

1) This paragraph provoked two adverse comments from participants. Professor de Bandt said that the national origin has "no significance at all in itself" as a criterion of adequacy "so long as the terms employed are not made more precise". Mr. Stepanek commented as follows: "It would be most foolish for at least half of the developing countries to try and obtain technological independence and have their technologies 'come from the country'. Most developing countries, including even India, do not yet have an operable capability to assess all the foreign technologies coming into the country. That would be the first objective which would be practical very soon for perhaps a dozen of the developing countries."

administrative, geological, geographical and other environment probably it might be considered as appropriate technology.

The second question was on what does the technology depend. The speakers came with many suggestions and it would appear that technology depends on many factors, such as income distribution, consumption patterns, economic infrastructure, etc. The determination of the appropriateness of any particular technology therefore becomes extremely difficult. It is probably the first time, however, that any concrete step has been taken to try to define the problem conceptually.

Another contribution I think was the discussion on whether it was possible to measure the appropriateness of a given technology. Many expert opinions were expressed and it was indicated by various eminent speakers that relative factor prices, elasticity of supply of labour and skills, size of the market and other variables like capital output ratios, capital labour ratios, labour output ratios, all had to be taken into account. It was also indicated that whatever criteria were applied, the appropriateness would have to be examined in the context of the prevailing economic system, and also of the relevant sector of the economy. For example, what is appropriate in the public sector need not be appropriate in the private sector; what is appropriate in a planned economy will probably not be appropriate in a free economy; what is appropriate in the metropolitan area will not be appropriate in rural areas. What is appropriate under certain conditions might not be appropriate in any other condition.

This makes it extremely difficult to measure the appropriateness of a technology. Will case studies offer any solutions? Will a matrix approach be helpful? The conclusion is that appropriateness of technology is an immeasurable concept. It can be intuitive rather than defined and put into a statistical matrix.

In that case what do we transfer? Transfer of technology was discussed in various contexts. If we are only thinking of importation of capital equipment, that is not transfer of technology. That is a transfer of capital equipment. Similarly the transfer of designs of blueprints, machines, or skilled workers or the importation of technical skills and training facilities, is not a transfer of technology. Technology is like a culture and no culture can be transported from one area to another. Therefore it can only be an intermingling of different technologies which makes adaptation difficult.

Another problem discussed was the role of international and national organisations. It is extremely difficult to say what their role is but this is probably the most vital question which we should face here. I am reminded of a sentence by Mr. Stepanek. "In an unofficial private capacity, I may say that I have been working underground." He may have said it in another context, but one thing is obvious - that the international organisations do not have any authority to direct any economy. They have to be persuasive, they have to work underground.

One of the expressions of working underground is that we have been collected here: we shall get some impressions, we shall establish some contacts and when we go back to our countries we shall have an impact. On the surface it may look a failure and I think Mr. Usui felt very pessimistic this morning about not having succeeded in getting the right impact. After some time, however, when we collect all the impressions that we have gained, we shall find that we have achieved very much. For example, without entering into the conflict between technologists and economists, one can say that this conference in itself is a contribution by bringing different currents of opinion together.

3. D. Carrière

It would be interesting, but it would take a very long time, to refer to all the themes which have been brought up during these three days. At various times we have talked about technology and production, technology and systems, technology and consumption, technology and the ideas of simplicity, technology and neutrality, of technology and historical evolution, to name only a few. But we also discussed technology and management capacity, technology and small, medium, and multinational enterprises, technology and market regulation, technology and management. In other words, the different schools of thought in this assembly expressed themselves through the medium of their own special interests in the area of technology.

A number of research subjects were put forward under Agenda Item A (Appropriate technology and development strategy), as is clear from the list I have just given. It became apparent that the internationalisation of the industrialisation process has been polarised around the large international companies, and that the technologies determined by the experts, on the basis of a voluminous literature, are oriented (and, in the extreme cases, imposed) by the big firms. I cite here the example of textiles, which Professor de Bandt has described to us. Another major concern of

Agenda Item A has been the myth - for I believe that it is a myth - of intermediate technology. I believe that we are in the process of dropping a concept which has caused torrents of ink to flow and consumed many tons of paper.

I now turn to Item B, which concerns policy appraisals at the national level. In this connection it is revealing to recall certain phrases of each of the speakers. Mr. Chesnais, of OECD, said that the social demand for science is not spontaneous, and demonstrated the need to centralise policies. A second point was raised by the UNESCO representative, who demonstrated the need to institute a dialogue between the scientific and technological community which does the work and the community of decision-makers, and especially the planners. Indeed, throughout the discussion, it seems that these different conceptions have brought out clearly one of the differences in approach which exist between us.

Mr. Gonod emphasised the importance of the definition of clear objectives. I would take this opportunity of saying that some of the objectives of this meeting have not been clearly enough stated for us to end up with very concrete proposals. Mr. Gonod also shed some light on communication difficulties between suppliers and users of technology, in his remarks on the dissatisfaction of sellers and users. Still on the problem of policy appraisal, I also noted Professor de Bandt's proposal to transfer a part of capital assistance to labour, but I will not retrace it in detail, since he has explained it much better than I could have done.

On the question of technological information for planning purposes, it was striking to note the lack of a system of statistics and indicators which would allow us to measure the development of technology. We listened carefully to the UNESCO representative's brilliant description of current studies of new sociocultural indicators, but I am very afraid that we will still have a long time to wait before this subject yields significant returns.

Noteworthy in Mr. Schweitzer's contribution was his statement that "the past explains the present". He emphasised the increasing need to employ succinct check-lists and matrix approaches.

For me, the most significant part of Mr. de Bandt's remarks lay in his attempt to demonstrate the possibility of optimum use of technology through an analysis of tasks and unit production costs. Very fortunately, he nevertheless concluded his discourse by telling us calculations must be confronted with the good sense of entrepreneurs.

Mr. Thoumi said one very important thing, which complements what I said previously about the power of negotiation - "the seller knows what he is selling, but the buyer doesn't know what he wants".

I was also very struck by Mr. Behari's remarks concerning the known constraints which operate. Mr. Behari told us that it was problems of adaptation that more directly affected his country, given the local materials and surpluses.

I will not dwell too long on the cost per branch, since it became quite clear that there were differences in concept between transfer of technology and transfer of information, or rather between transfer of know-how and knowledge and transfer of information, depending on the one hand on the technology used, and on the other, on the branch of industry involved. Throughout these sessions, we have been discussing rural enterprises and handicrafts in addition to small and medium industries and multinational enterprises. The whole of this part was most interesting, but would require a much longer and much more specialised debate between people speaking the same language.

I would now very quickly like to give you my general impressions. One would have imagined that both the suppliers and the buyers of technology would have attended this meeting. In fact, the suppliers of technology were not officially represented. The users were represented at the level of national or regional public bodies dealing with industrial development. Finally, in greatest numbers, were those from a third category, researchers and advisors, who themselves split into two categories, the technicians and the economists. In this connection, it is revealing to note that today the technicians are making use in their research of sociological and psycho-sociological notions, while the economists show a more marked tendency to use formulas and mathematical models. I think it is a good thing, for it indicates that the trend of several years ago is now being reversed.

Many ideas have come out of this meeting, but there were some oversights, of which I would cite two: first, in my opinion, was the absence of a debate at the level of the actors and factors involved in the adaptation and choice of technologies.

We said very little, except a few words this morning on the problems of "communicability" - especially of migrants. The second omission, surprisingly enough, was the failure to discuss the two major experiments, those of Japan and China.

In our discussion, the problem of information seemed to raise the most difficulties. I won't dwell any longer on this, for the discussion is fresh, and it is still buzzing in your ears. Technology seems inseparable from the market, but we have found that in many cases, the multinational companies prefabricate the demand. Generally, in all the discussions, there has been confusion between channels of information and their content. The measures already taken by developing countries tend to prove that they are mature and able to make their own adaptations. They look for progress solely in the possibilities of choice offered by the wealthy nations. The most important lesson drawn here was that case studies generally produce the best results.

Finally, a brief description of a few concrete proposals which seem to have emerged from this meeting. I did not attend the second part of this morning's meeting, but I have been informed that the International Institute of Industrial Development described by Mr. Stepanek showed definite promise. It would certainly be useful for the OECD Development Centre to review this question with UNIDO.

I believe that among the themes we have discussed during this meeting, we should retain for future research: a better understanding of the actors in the choice and adaptation of technologies and the study of "communicability" at different levels, particularly at the planning level and at the enterprise level.

It would be necessary to focus in depth on this problem in order to identify those factors which restrain this communication. It is not a question of creating yet another structure, but rather of launching a movement of stimulation, concerted action, and demonstration in order that developing countries may have genuine access to all the sources and possibilities of information.

4. N. de Figueiredo

I will not try to present any summary of conclusions of the proceedings. It would not be possible, nor perhaps useful. Instead I will present what I would call my own personal conclusions in relation to the many points discussed during the meeting. Of course, these conclusions are basically influenced by my previous experience as well as by my present interests. This means that they are of course biased in the sense that they are conclusions that I have derived from the point of view of my own professional interests at the moment. I think perhaps it will be useful.

I have nine points I would like to make. The first relates to the central subject of this meeting: the choice and adaptation of technology. My impression is that this subject must be viewed

within a general context of cultural change. I think it is very
clear from the discussions that an isolated conception of choice
and adaptation of techniques is not in order. I would say that
choice and adaptation of techniques are an integral part of a
natural process, the process of cultural change. This has certain
implications. One is that one must separate what is a problem of
training, of acquiring skills that are needed to adopt the technologies required by modern industrial development, from the problem we discussed here of adaptation of technology. I feel that we
must separate both these in order not to confuse the subject. One
thing is just to upgrade the local skills in order to be able to
absorb the techniques that are available and that are needed for
modern industrial development. And a quite different thing is to
adapt a technique and to choose techniques from the available
reservoir in order to meet the requirements in developing countries.

A second point is that we must discuss and deal with this
subject in a more flexible way, in the sense that there is a process of reciprocal adaptation between the environment on one side
and the techniques on the other side. This means that there is no
process of unilateral transfer of techniques from abroad and of
absorption of these techniques. Instead, there is a reciprocal
process, of adaptation of techniques on the one hand and of change
of institutions, of change of values, and of change of inputs to
fit the requirements of the new techniques.

A third point is a point that was mentioned by Mr. Ikonicoff.
I think he is entirely right in saying that the problems of transfer of technology, of adaptation of technology, arise mostly because the techniques arrive in an industrial environment that
responds to entirely different social systems; there is no use in
trying to find a solution without taking into consideration this
basic dichotomy. Of course, the factor proportions in the available
techniques in the more developed countries are not adapted to the
factor proportions in the developing countries. The needs in relation to techniques in developing countries are mostly influenced
by the pattern of consumption which is influenced by demonstration
effects from the developed countries. I think that this must be
taken for granted and there is no use in trying to find ways and
means to change these basic facts. It is a fact of life and it
means on the one hand that education, the system of values and
even the resource endowment of the developing countries must be
adjusted with time to the requirements of technology arising from
the developed countries' techniques. On the other hand, these

techniques of course must also be adapted to the socio-economic environment prevailing in the developing countries. There is thus a reciprocal adjustment process as I mentioned before.

Another point I should like to mention is that I believe that policies influencing the choice and the adaptation of techniques should be designed mostly with a view to increasing efficiency at the plant level and not directly to increasing employment. Employment is important but I think that the employment objective should be taken care of through national economic policies influencing, at the macro level, the capital output ratio, the allocation of resources, etc.

My fifth point I suppose is related to the statements which were made by various speakers on the different sectors and branches of activity. It is clear to me that, with the exception of construction, in all branches of activity that were considered, there are no clear alternative techniques[1]. This means that given the production function, and level of efficiency there are basically no widely differing alternatives of production. Another possible exception mentioned, apart from construction, which shattered my previous views on the matter is related to chemical industries. I was most impressed by Mr. Giral's exposé and paper. It is a belief, I suppose, of nearly every economist that the continuous process industries offer less alternatives with regard to techniques. Economists accept that there may be alternative techniques for example, in the textile industry, in the non-continuous process industries, etc. but not in the chemical industry. I suppose that nearly all economists believe that the chemical industries use monolithic technologies which one has to accept exist in the developed countries, or completely reject; not change or adapt.

The next point is related to information services. I shall briefly say some words on the usefulness of a high degree of centralisation of such services. Broadly speaking a high degree of centralisation could be useful for data of a more general character, say, profiles that are needed for programming. Such data were, in the past, actively prepared by the United Nations. Now that there is a slowing down in this activity I think it would be useful for others to start again collecting this kind of data. However, I do not see the possibility of gathering plant level data on a multi-

1) Professor de Bandt points out that this conclusion would not be accepted by most participants and does not seem to reflect the Group's discussions of different sectors.

lateral basis. I share the view that this is basically a national responsibility. Each country should, either on a centralised basis, or on a decentralised basis as is done by big countries like India or Brazil, collect data in the form which is the most adequate in relation to each branch of industry.

I would also like to point out that in my view it would be most useful if the information services were part of the research institutes, both because in this way the research institutes would perform a function of feeding these information services and also because the information services then would perform the most useful function of a bridge between the research institutes and private industry. The two institutions would thus complement each other.

My next point is a remark on the absence of reference in the meeting, and also in the agenda, to development financing agencies as instruments for the choice and adaptation of techniques. In recent years, the financial agencies have been moving more and more towards technical assistance activities as a parallel to their financing activities. Even the conservative World Bank is now giving important technical assistance. I think that the financing agencies, as they are in some cases already doing, could perform a useful role in two aspects. First, they could complement the financial and economic analysis of the project by an analysis of the technological aspects of the project. This means evaluating the technology in each project. Second, they could extend technical assistance. This means giving technical assistance in a way that is most common in agriculture, where credit is often extended with a package of technical services and technical assistance. This is already done in Brazil and I think that it is a most useful implement. It should be considered as a practical proposal for, I would say, every country.

My next point relates to something that appears to me to be very helpful. It is another absence in the discussions – the absence of an obstacle to the transfer of technology as represented by the high cost of technology. There is a widespread belief that the high cost of technology is an important obstacle to its diffusion. I believe that cost is not a problem. Ignorance, lack of knowledge, lack of bargaining power are more important obstacles and as a result of this the cost may be up. In a non-monopolistic market, however, I think that experience shows that cost is not by itself an obstacle to the transfer of technology. And the fact that cost was not mentioned as an obstacle in our discussions, I suppose, is helpful.

My ninth and last point concerns research priorities. The agenda appears to be based on the assumption that it should be possible to prepare some research list, some shopping list of research priorities in the field of adaptation of technologies, perhaps, by branch of industry. From the discussions, however, it appears that no such list exists. That is, in the discussions of different branches of activity no such priorities appeared in the sense that the research priorities were not specific to the developing countries. Now this is exactly my point. Of course there are research priorities, but these research priorities apply simultaneously mostly both to developed and to developing countries. It is very difficult to establish two lists, one list of research priorities for developed countries and another list for developing countries. It appears to me that there is a large overlapping margin. What is needed by the developing countries is often also needed by the developed countries. The reason is that the basic and the applied research that is needed for certain development, e.g. to develop a certain innovation, is equally needed for the development of some other innovations some of which are useful to developed countries and some of which are useful to developing countries. I will give you two brief examples.

Two or three years ago, the United States Government convened an international conference on nutrition. When this conference ended there appeared a list of priorities for action by the U.S. Government in favour of LDCs. On the top of this list was research to develop new sources of protein foods. This was mentioned as a basic need for developing countries. It is also a basic need of the U.S., however. There is the nutrition problem in certain regions of that country and among certain minorities of its population. It is startling, but most of the problems that could be listed as priority problems in the developing countries are in one way or another also basic problems of the developed countries.

Another example is this. Mr. Schweitzer mentioned the experience that was made by NASA trying to transfer innovations developed in the U.S. for the spatial programme, to the developing countries. He mentioned the case of Korea. A similar exercise was done with Brazil some years ago, exactly in the same way as he described(1). Several topics were selected and four or five items of innovation resulting from the NASA programme were transferred to Brazil and

_____

1) Mr. Schweitzer comments that "the Brazil experience has no relevance to the Korea experiment".

are being **applied**. One is the application of infra-red aerial
photography which allows very efficient surveys of natural resources.
I suppose it was the first time that it was done in a developing
country. It was developed by NASA and it is being applied extensively in Brazil in the Amazon region since last year. This shows
that a separation between research needs of developing countries
and the research needs of the developed ones is somewhat difficult
to justify. There is a margin of overlapping which I think is substantial.

5. J. Giral B.

I will try not to duplicate and will just go through the
points that were not touched, or where the emphasis I would like
to place on them is different. On the matter of appropriate technology and development strategy, I think that the semantics of
whether "intermediate", "appropriate", "convergent", "adequate",
etc. are important and I agree with Mrs. Stewart that something
ought to be done, not only at the level of defining this term but
a full glossary of terms for this potential of adaptation. Many of
these terms we have believed in, I saresay, carelessly, and we
should be trying to be more specific. This is something OECD, perhaps, could do.

I was impressed by Mr. Usui's comments on Ranis' paper about
the economies of scale being often exaggerated. Small and medium
industries adapt more easily and contribute in countries such as
Japan substantially to the national product and exports. I think
this is something to keep in mind. We tend to be overwhelmed by
the phantom of the scale problem.

The experience of India is a very important one that should
be disseminated and studied more carefully, so that other countries
benefit from it. I on my part will ask formally Messrs. Behari and
Nanjappa to establish a good communication channel with us in
Mexico and I will get to that later.

The transfer and adaptation of technology through the multi-
national corporations was discussed lightly. Obviously there are
many pro's and con's, but this is an area that merits deeper study
in my opinion.

Policy appraisals at the national level. This being a fashion-
able thing today, i.e. countries making new policies to protect and
promote industrialisation, research, exports, import substitution,
registers of technology, limits for negotiation, etc. I think it
is important to be aware of the tremendous influence, as Mr. Goulet

pointed out, that directly and indirectly, these policies have in the way technology is used (selected, transferred, adapted, implemented). This is another area that deserves further study, and I am glad to see that Mr. Usui has it in his programme.

I would like to cover points (C) and (D) together, because I feel methodology and availability of information go together. I think there was a general consensus as to the fact that we all could benefit from more information. I think also this is where the consensus ended. Therefore, rather than trying to interpret the feeling of the majority, I think at least I will be coherent if I give my own version: We need to analyse the problem better. Call it epistemology, morphological analysis or plain common sense, we have to identify the problem. A very rough structure, to go quickly through it. What are the needs? Who are the end-users? How technically prepared are they? What do they want? As Mr. Teitel pointed out, do they want an idea, a pre-investment study, a process selection study, a project, a process optimisation, a technical detail, the whole thing, stock and barrel? What is really what they want, and at what level should we address the problem?

What does each country need? By sector, by region, etc.

What are the disciplines involved? By subjects, what types of pieces of information? What types of packages to transfer the information? Who has them and who needs them? How can it be transferred? Channels, costs, prices. I think there is a difference between the price one has to pay explicitly, and the implicit cost of breaking the semantics barriers to opening this communications channel. Once all this is done, I think we can begin to address ourselves to the problem: What are the approaches? Are there any methodologies successful in one case that could be applied to other problems? Are there any common denominators in technical skills that merit suggesting a training programme, either at university level or as independent programme or any other way? Are there common needs of information not covered by the existing information systems that would justify creation of new systems, with the logistics and the costs of creating new information systems?

On this morning's session I was particularly impressed by Mr. Harper's thought-provoking talk. If we all realise the tremendous effort it takes to select, transfer, and adapt technology, how much can we afford to make the same mistakes as industrialised countries and compound them with our own mistakes? At the same time, how much can we afford to stop and think about designing a

- 129 -

new "development concept" when all around us there is a feeling
of urgency? I would like to emphasise the importance of paying
serious attention to these concepts and of not just storing them
as a nice piece of social conversation. Perhaps the concept of
"soft" technology in the meaning of "non-capital" technology could
be one of the partial solutions.

As a Latin American, I want to use my last minutes to
Mr. Gonod's comments on the OAS project, which deserves all my
respect. If one could organise around such a backbone regional
project other loose efforts we are all doing all over the world,
I think we could triple the effectiveness of the resources applied.
Also, such a consolidation of efforts would allow us to go much
further ahead in given directions provided that we chose the right
directions to go.

6. **M.A.M.** Shabaan

I would like to start by saying that the diversification of
discussion, which some of our friends have referred to, is a very
healthy sign of the success of this meeting. In fact we are people
representing various corners of the earth who have come here to
discuss a very important subject which is very vague in its nature
and very difficult to reach a final conclusion about. Therefore,
I think it would have been far-fetched if anyone had expected that,
in two and a half days, we were going to come out with a number of
resolutions.

Having said this, my first point is on the meaning of the
word "technology". It was mentioned that when we discuss technology we must consider not only the manufacturing process but also
know-how maintenance, management know-how and sales know-how. I
think this is very important because no industry can achieve any
success without effective know-how in all these areas. I would
also like to stress the importance of adequate training facilities
for the developing countries in this field, and in addition, subscribe to what was said earlier about the training of personnel
for industrial planning, for the choice of manufacturing process
and for price negotiations in connection with the transfer of
technologies.

The next point I should like to make is nomenclature with
respect to "intermediate technology", "convenient technology",
"optimum technology", "appropriate technology". What do we want?
We want the "correct technology" for the environment prevailing
in a certain part of the world. This correct technology is best

described as "appropriate" technology. I think the word "appropriate" is very useful and I think that it covers what we want to say. Appropriate technology must be subject to the prevailing local conditions which are influenced by a number of factors as, for example, the inputs of the industry. What sort of raw materials are available in the area? If available raw materials can be used with process A but not with process B one would have to adopt process A. Is power available at a cheap cost or not? Is water available in plentiful quantities? All such local factors affect also the choice of the process.

A great deal has been said about the pattern of consumption and I think that this is very important. The consumption of developed countries in, say, a product like plastics differs very much from that of developing countries. Social conditions, financial conditions, manpower, all these factors plus others to be mentioned must be the basis for the choice of technology. Needless to say, all the technical people here know that very sophisticated industries need first-class labour which might not always be available in a developing country.

The next point, although it does not apply to my country, is on the cost of transfer of technology, together with the availability of the know-how. I know from personal experience with neighbouring countries who ask for our help that this is cause for great difficulties. As Mr. Stepanek said, some countries are victimised in this respect. This is quite clear because if somebody wants to buy a commodity which he does not know anything about, the salesman might say that the cost is 10, when the real price is only 7. In this respect I must say that UNIDO has been of some service. They have published a number of books which, I think, can serve as profiles for industrialisation in some developing countries.

It is, needless to say, that to transfer the knowledge which would help developing countries to plan better, is not an easy job. I realise that it would be a great burden on any organisation to take up this responsibility. However, the assistance which is given is helpful and represents a step in the right direction.

Another very interesting point which was mentioned was the experience of Argentina regarding the local manufacture of some of its requirements like transistors, etc., and I would like to say that we in Egypt have also gone through a similar experience. We have been able to pulp very low quality cellulose products and we mix four parts of this pulp with one part of imported material to produce our own writing paper. The plant is supposed to be the first of its kind in the world. This should give encouragement to some developing countries, by showing that we can also do something on our own and need not entirely rely on external sources for information about know-how or technology.

The concept of soft technology is very attractive and the way it was explained makes me believe that the Organisation should give more emphasis to soft technology. I think that a development of this branch of technology could help the developing countries very much to improve their standards of living and this is the aim of all the organisations of the world. To me, it should be given priority number one on the list of future subjects to be handled by the Organisation.

In connection with a case I know of, a plant in a neighbouring country, I should again like to stress the importance of training. The productivity of this plant was one sixth of its rated capacity. When I went to investigate it I found out that the reason was bad maintenance. Most of the developing countries give importance to some simple training for the production personnel. They attach very little importance, however, to maintenance and they do not seem to think of its effect on the production costs.

Good management is another very important question and I think any international organisation that gives emphasis to this subject would render great service to the developing countries.

In conclusion, I must say I am optimistic, and I think that when we are all back home we are going to confer with our colleagues about the proceedings of this meeting and I am sure in the very near future we shall receive from each other more crystalised ideas about the subject. If we cannot come out with definite and clear resolutions, it does not mean at all that the meeting was not a success. I would like to end by thanking the Organisation for giving me a chance to meet our excellent and esteemed colleagues here. Thank you.

7. S. Teitel

Fortunately for me I have been preceded by so many brilliant friends and rapporteurs that they left little for me to say, and I would try to avoid going into too much detail. In the first place I would like to start by saying that the secretariat of this meeting has to be congratulated, because they managed to convene such a meeting and to reach this point under very severe constraints, I would say, from the point of view of the knowledge we have in the area and given the time for preparation.

I would allow myself to be a little bit critical, also, and
I would like to start by saying that the first point raised which
I would like to highlight, was problem definition. My own conclusion, I must say, was that it was not tackled to my satisfaction.
The sort of implicit assumption I detected around the table seems
to me, with few exceptions of course, that (to paraphrase it) we
were saying to the people in developing countries: "You do not
really know what to produce and how to produce, and it is our duty
to tell you what to do and how to do it". On the question of nomenclature, which I also think is very important, although for slightly
different reasons, I would like to quote to you the words of a
famous expert on the choice and adaptation of technology who said:

> "Here is glory for you".
> "I don't know what you mean by glory", Alice said.
> "I meant 'there is a nice argument for you'".
> "But 'glory' does not mean a nice argument", Alice objected.
> "When I use a word", Humpty Dumpty said in a rather scornful
> tone, "it means just what I choose it to mean, no more, no
> less."

Another point which was stressed again and again seemed to be
that more and more information is required, without particularly
caring to define information for what or for whom. In this connection, also, questions of secrecy, obstacles and high cost were
raised about this still undefined information. This seemed to be
a little bit out of focus, consequently.

The issue of the development of small-scale industries and the
improvement of industrial extension services, both to literate and
illiterate entrepreneurs, was raised and it seemed to me to be very
relevant. However, again a little bit out of place. Why? Because
it has been treated extensively elsewhere at many other meetings
and is well covered in the literature, including the literature of
this House.

It was apparent to me from the rather scarce statements coming
from those people who have tried to move one step beyond their own
rationalisations of the problem, that they found reality to be quite
different. People are generally not fools, and the distribution of
wealth is generally not directly correlated to that of ability and
intelligence. They do sensible things in relation to the environment
and to their resources and in general to the signals they get from
the outside world.

Another issue about which we talked only very little, and which concerns me a great deal, is the lack of a common language among the participants, due to differences in background, training, as well as experience. I would say again that this makes the need to devote some effort to questions of nomenclature even more relevant.

The few examples of industry and other sector studies presented, showed a rather low level of methodological skill - a clear reflection of the learning process which the "experts" are undergoing.

In the final session, the question was raised of the neutrality of technology with reference to our value system, as if technology were not applicable to human objectives but as if there were a necessary complementarity between the hardness of the technology and the prevailing socio-economic political system. This issue, while of great importance, and carefully avoided so far by most social scientists, seems to me again rather out of place for this meeting, which was convened for a rather more specific and narrowly defined purpose.

Finally, I would say that a positive, as opposed to a normative look at our discussions and problems would lead to the following conclusions. What is required is apparently an improvement of the knowledge and skill in the developing countries to adapt and obtain technology. Consequently, there are no short-cuts, no gimmicks, no packages here. This demands:

i) building the necessary infrastructure in the developing
    countries, which includes educational, scientific and
    technical services, including information, consultance
    and other industry related services; for example, there
    is mention of the difficulty with tools and dyes in metal-
    working; it is not a question of a package of technology
    which is incomplete if you just have people trained in
    industrial schools who know how to draw and you just
    produce draftsmen, but if you produce an educational school
    for tool and dyemakers, this solves your problem; you must
    first copy and then you create your tools and dyes;

ii) acquiring the political will to bargain and to get better
    services and terms.

In conclusion, Mr. Chairman, I would like to quote another expert in the choice and adaptation of technology, who said something which in my mind is relevant to our whole discussion. "Not only is there but one way of doing things rightly, but there is only one way of seeing them and that is seeing the whole of them". Thank you Mr. Chairman.

8. J. Stepanek(1)

Thank you Mr. Chairman. I accepted the task today for which I was asked to volunteer from the point of view of identifying points made during the last three days that I thought you might want to include in your proceedings and might be worth reading one year from today. Now, even with this harsh criterion, I suggested to myself yesterday that, there might be six such points. My studies last night identified about 20(1). Thank goodness, though, most have already been stated, so don't worry. But on that criterion, I would like to say that this meeting has been a success, if I am correct in saying that there are as many as 20 points made. Let me start to give you just a sample.

First, I think that most of us have forgotten (including the speaker) what the real basic objective of this meeting is. It is not technology. Technology is a means to something else, which was clearly stated in paragraph 1 of the background to the Aide Memoire, where it was stated: "... the overriding problems are unemployment, utilisation of local resources and income distribution". Now, whether we concur that these are basic objectives or not, I do suggest to the management that in the proceedings we clearly state what brought us together.

Second, we have implied in much of our discussion, without clearly stating, the relationship between our objectives and the title of this meeting - adaptation and choice of technology - and I would suggest that there is a little bridge there which can be easily abstracted out of the discussion.

Third, I revert to the question of definition. I know we have heard of it a lot. I do have now a firm recommendation to make. "Intermediate technology" describes a group of technologies which I could take my camera and photograph. "Appropriate technology" describes not a technology at all, but a concept that I could not photograph. I think this is to me a distinction, and the Indians invented the word "appropriate" technology, so I think that Mr. Nanjappa, Mr. Behari and I can speak with a little authority

---

1) Mr. Stepanek submitted a comprehensive summary of his conclusions which has been placed immediately after this statement.

on that subject. Now, unfortunately, both the terms "intermediate" and "appropriate" are not wholly acceptable. I suggest instead such a phrase as "the appropriate choice of technology", which is a politically acceptable word through market tests in many countries. Also this brings us down to the real world of the moment, because in 1972 people over the developing world will be deciding on the technology to the extent of ∅10 billion. This is roughly the investment in machinery and equipment and the technologies required to put them into operation. This no way implies that the choice should be limited, and I agree with Mrs. Stewart that you might prefer widening this a little by just saying you "widen the appropriate choice of technology", if that would cover the fact that we do not want to limit ourselves to the technologies of the present.

A lot has been said about government policy already. We will skip that. There is need for new strategies, which are very important, and about which we said a lot.

It was pointed out in respect to international companies that they had, from the evidence given, a very high potential for designing new technologies, but we also have evidence that this is generally not being utilised at present. Similarly, for UNIDO, there is an unrealised potential for improvement or adaptation of the technologies put into use which could be realised through some changes. I would hope that this meeting would want to say something on that subject.

I came to the conclusion from this meeting that generally we are underestimating the value of consulting companies. And I think that this is a very important conclusion, if you think it is a conclusion. On the other hand, I think over the past years we have grossly overestimated the value of industrial research. I am sorry to say that because my background is in industrial research. In the future, in the words of Schweitzer, we might pay more attention to the extension of the research than to just piling up more research which is not put to use. I might remind you also that consulting work is a capital-saving type of activity, whereas industrial research is a capital-using type of activity.

And so on and so on. I think we can build up a rather interesting and variable presentation, which I know that we in UNIDO will look forward to with very great interest. Coming from OECD - an objective group - I am sure that UNIDO's management will be paying attention to it. Thank you very much Mr. President for the opportunity we have had to participate in this very very interesting meeting.

Written Submission of his Conclusions

Basic Problem. Unemployment is becoming the outstanding problem of many developing countries.

Growing unemployment is the result of many factors such as low rates of economic growth, differential rates of growth between the modern and traditional sectors, increasing rates of entry into the labour force, and over-dependence upon technologies designed to save labour. (The influence of each of the factors on employment for specific countries is generally not known and is an important question to be studied.) Any attack on the unemployment problem thus requires attention to more than the technology factor.

Definitions. The actions to be taken to improve the value of industrial technologies to the developing countries in such a way that the pressure of unemployment might be relieved were described in various ways. By some, the term "intermediate technology" is used to define a group of technologies intermediate in cost per work place between the most modern and the most traditional. Others use "appropriate technology" to describe the concept that each technology should be appropriately designed and/or selected for the social and economic conditions at the point of use. (Generally now technologies are designed for their point of origin which in most cases is in an industrial country with quite different social and economic conditions prevailing.) One participant described a pragmatic approach in which "convenient technologies" were used with considerable success. Another participant directed attention to the "choice" as the critical factor and suggested the descriptive phrase "appropriate choice of technology". If the "choice" was too narrow then new technologies would have to be developed through adaptation or invention. Most participants agreed that the term "technology" should be used in a broad sense and, for example, should include "management" and other "social" technologies.

Government Policies and Actions. The policies which governments pursue with respect to industrialisation are the key factors with respect to the technological choices. In many cases governments are still favouring the import of labour saving technologies and in such cases activities to develop indigenous and more appropriate technologies might not be fully effective. However, increasingly policy revaluations are being made by governments with respect to technology utilisation under the impact of growing unemployment.

To affect significantly unemployment through technological changes, many of the participants felt, revolutionary changes might have to be made in government policies and in the prevailing capital cost per unit of production. (An approximate 10 to 1 reduction might have to be attempted.) At the same time, the industrialisation strategy would have to cover a different product mix.

Shadow pricing, or industrialisation policies which converted shadow prices into market prices, generally modify the choice of technologies and could improve the rate of employment.

As per capita incomes increase in the developing countries and approach those in the industrial countries, it is likely that new consumption patterns will develop and as a result a different mix of technologies will be required.

The introduction of new technologies other than the so-called modern western technologies, has to overcome a feeling that the former might be second class or inferior, and an educational campaign may be essential.

Thus, non-economic factors, such as an acquired taste for foreign products or foreign levels of quality, influence the technology. Sugar was given as an example. The choice of a technology is closely related to capital inflow. Were a country to wish to become independent of foreign technologies then it would have almost to become independent of foreign capital flows.

The very rapid rate of urbanisation in a number of the developing countries makes imperative the need for new technologies. Not only must employment be provided but inexpensive food process--ing technologies are required to feed the urban populations. One suggestion was made that it might be necessary to subsidise initially the commercialisation of such technologies.

Technology adaptation. The potential for technological adaptation has generally been underestimated because of the overwhelming commitment to the present labour saving technologies. Most of the participants were able to give evidence of successful technological adaptations even including the chemical process technologies which are generally considered to be inflexible with respect to capital and labour utilisation.

Evidence was made available by a number of participants that the range of technologies available is already wide, particularly for the metal processing industries. Thus it is possible at present to improve the choice of technologies with respect to the local environment.

Emphasis was made by a number of participants that the so-called "simple" technologies which are urgently required need a higher level of technical skill for their design and implementation than even the more sophisticated technologies. Information was presented on relatively rapid rates of employment increase through a technologi al dification in the Indian soap industry.

Examples were also given of technological adaptations of traditional technologies, for example in brick making, which resulted in higher costs of production and were therefore not acceptable.

The suggestion was made that the lack of technological self-sufficiency could be measured by the number of "package plants" imported.

The construction industry in general and housing in particular were considered areas for technological adaptation and considerable experience was cited.

Industrial Information. The participants agreed that one of the most important actions to be taken to improve the technologies employed was to acquire access to industrial information. A distinction was made between information publicly available and proprietary information. While considerable concern was expressed at the high cost of proprietary information and the difficulty in negotiating for privately held technologies, there was also a realisation that public information was being inadequately utilised. A number of examples were given of new technologies developed through access to public information alone. A number of participants, e.g. from Mexico, described their national information services.

Many of the participants expressed appreciation of the UNIDO question and answer service and felt that the newly established equipment information service could be most important to them in the future. Only one participant felt that the UNIDO enquiry service had not been adequate to his needs.

Many of the participants questioned the recent termination of the information service by the OECD Development Centre.

Industrial Research. Most of the participants felt that industrial research institutes have a potential not now being realised, not so much through a lack of research capability but through an inability to extend research results into commercial enterprises. The conclusion was that industrial research institutes should now spend considerable additional attention on extension activities.

One participant mentioned that an industrial research institute in a developing country was considered remote and foreign to most industrialists and was not considered practical by them. His conclusion was that business oriented consulting services by research institutes would have to be emphasised.

An example was given of an experiment to transfer and to use commercially highly sophisticated space research from an industrial country into an industrialising country. The experiment, which at first identified approximately 150 potential applications was able to implement four to five in the form of new products. The cost of this experimental project was justified not only by the new products introduced, but by the methodologies for transfer which were developed.

National Consulting Companies. The potential of consulting companies, particularly those covering engineering services, has not been fully realised in the developing countries and priority should be given to the establishment of such firms. Evidence was given of the considerable adaptation of technologies possible through the work of designers in such companies. National consulting companies can become one of the main points of entry of new technologies into the country while at the same time adapting them to the needs of the country. Governments can assist by making loans available to national companies which wish to use consulting organisations.

International Companies. International companies have the capability to modify technologies, as was made evident by a number of examples. However, as a whole, international companies tend to transfer technologies without modification. Neither do they transfer the ability to generate new national technologies[1].

UNIDO Work Programme. A number of participants noted that the UNIDO Work Programme was mainly engaged in the transfer of technologies, but with little adaptation. Note was made that in general the recipients of UNIDO technical assistance wish to have the most modern technologies without modification. It was further pointed out that were the market demand to change, UNIDO on short notice would be able to initiate programmes of technology adaptation on a much larger scale.

---

1) G. Boon sent the following comments on this particular passage:
    "I am in disagreement with the statements. The multinational firm wants, generally speaking, to increase its rate of return on its investment. Therefore, it is interested in cost minimisation, and, due to an often larger arsenal of intellectual and practical experiences compared with the local firm, it may do a better job in the selection and adaptation area. The last sentence of this paragraph is also not necessarily true; on the contrary, the multinational firm may set an example on appropriate technology choice and adaptations to national firms. The latter firms have often more feelings for prestige and other extra-economic considerations concerning technology than the multinational firm has."
    See also Part One, Chapter III.

II. <u>WRITTEN SUBMISSIONS REVIEWING OR SUPPLEMENTING THE DISCUSSION</u>

1. Peter Harper: Soft Technology(1)

"Soft technology" is not a well-defined term. It means different things to different proponents (and opponents). It also has mixed goals, aiming at the maximisation of a number of different variables on the supposition that they are likely to be related, or at least not incompatible. These diverse goals are cemented together by diffuse ideological convictions about the working of natural systems, the use of natural resources, the preconditions of work-satisfaction, the control of technology and so on: in fact, the nature of the Good Life. A large part of this ideological backcloth would appear to originate in the last decade's upsurge of criticism of modern science and technology, which has been remarkably diverse(2).

Because the term "soft technology" is so vague it is hard to discuss directly. Instead I propose to break the idea down into various of its goals. The technology associated with each individual goal can be discussed more easily. Often the phrase "alternative technologies" is used to refer to these(3). This usage has terminological difficulties in common with the term "appropriate technologies in begging the question ("appropriate to what?" - "alternative to what?"). Technologies can be "appropriate" or "alternative" in

---

1) This note is a slightly condensed version of the essay contributed by Peter Harper.

2) For a sample, see J. Ellul, <u>The Technological Society</u> (Knopf, 1964); Herbert Marcuse, <u>One-Dimensional Man</u> (Sphere, London, 1969); John McDermott, "Technology, the Opiate of the Intellectuals", <u>New York Review of Books</u>, 13, (2), (1969); Lewis Mumford, <u>The Pentagon of Power</u>, Harcourt, Brace and Jovanovich, 1970; J.R. Ravetz, <u>Scientific Knowledge and its Social Problems</u> (Oxford U.P. 1971); and Theodore Roszak, <u>The Making of a Counter-Culture</u> (Faber, 1969).

3) Sometimes "Alternative Technology" is used interchangeably with "soft technology" in meaning "environmentally sound technology", or even a similar kind of mixture to soft technology. The Movement is not noted for its semantic hygiene. Further discussion of alternative technologies can be found in Peter Harper and Björn Eriksson, "Alternative Technology: A Guide to Sources and Contacts", <u>Undercurrents No.3</u> (1972), 34, Cholmley Gardens, Aldred Road, London, N.W.6.

so many ways. In fact the meaning becomes established by convention within the community that uses it. So, the term "alternative technology" has acquired an 'illicit' content narrower than a strict interpretation would call for: thus not all technical alternatives to existing technology are called by the name. As I have heard the term used, the content seems to be conditioned by the connotations of the word "alternative" in the 'counter-culture' (youth culture) of the West: not controlled by dominant institutions, cheap, improvisatory, personalised, accessible to amateurs. Not surprisingly, the literature of alternative technology, such as it is, tends not to be very accessible in the academic, governmental or business subcultures.

Alternative to what? The scope of the term "technology" is generally taken broadly. At the narrowest we could mean just hardware, at the broadest, with Frances Stewart, we could mean methods of production taken together. Many of the alternatives are technically quite orthodox, but the manner in which they are organised may be different (e.g. "communal" factories). In other cases the manner of organisation may be quite usual, but the techniques are not (e.g. the aquaculture-horticulture rotation system developed by the New Alchemy Institute on Cape Cod, U.S.A.). In yet other cases the unorthodoxy lies merely in not using the technique which is most efficient, for "non-economic" reasons. The orthodoxy is generally identified as highly centralised large-scale, automated production systems requiring a high level of expertise and deep division of labour, good process control, consuming large quantities of non-renewable materials and energy and seemingly requiring extensive control of personnel, markets and sources of supply.

There is a growing critical literature about such systems. Some feel that they are intrinsically "dehumanising", "alienating", etc. Others consider that they inevitably lead to such problems as depletion of resources, damage to the environment, exploitation of one area or group by another, dangerous possibilities of mis-use, etc. to a degree sufficient to outweigh their undoubted advantages in other respects. To the extent that such vast technological production systems can be identified with capitalism, the Marxist and para-Marxist literature has always been critical, but has only recently turned its attention to the technical aspects apart from the purely social and political ones. Solutions offered are varied of course, and are a mixture of social and technological suggestions. What seems to be new, and justifies speaking of "alternative technologies" as a separate category, is the increasing emphasis on

technical matters, and a recognition that the methods of production
are a vital part of what it feels like to live in a particular
society, and are in that sense political matters. There are technological constraints, but there are no technological imperatives.

Different types of alternative technologies are best identifiable in terms of the communities that formulate and practice them.
Sometimes they state their goals and assumptions clearly; more
generally they do not. On the whole, little attempt is made to cast
the goals into a set of operational rules that an engineer might
follow. Instead, practitioners are expected to judge intuitively
whether a given line of development accords with the goals.

Classification of alternative technologies is difficult because in reality all groups have mixed goals. Here are some typical
expressed goals:

- regional self-sufficiency
- resource conservation
- direct control by producers and consumers
- absence of exploitation
- ecological stability
- satisfaction in production process
- recovery after "apocalypse".

The supposition is that such goals cannot only be sought by
social policy, but that certain types of technology are more or
less appropriate to them, and that these could or should be insti-
tuted along with the social factors. It is easy to imagine that
there may be technologies appropriate to single quantifiable goals
(that, in the view of the critics, is partly the trouble), but
where there are mixed goals, conflicts arise and there can be very
strong divergencies in how these conflicts are resolved.

Ecological Technology. This is a strong component of many
alternative technologies, and many people use the term "soft technology" to refer to it. There are any number of approaches to it,
depending on various ecological theories. Of course, plenty of
purely technical solutions have been put forward in a perfectly
orthodox way by big manufacturing corporations, but for present
purposes these do not count. Somewhat more radical are proposals
such as those of Commoner(1) to substitute a fixed catalogue of
environmentally damaging technologies (such as the private auto-
mobile, chemical fertilisers, chemical pesticides) with "clean

---

1) Barry Commoner, The Closing Circle, Cape 1972.

technologies" doing essentially the same thing (such as public
transport, "organic" fertilisers, biological pest control) some of
which may have strong implications for work organisation. A more
catastrophic view of ecological stability sees the causes of environmental deterioration in globally cumulative deviations from
"natural" ecological cycles. The only guaranteed security lies in
a technology that mimics these cycles to within some supposed
homeostatic tolerance. This leads to very decentralised communities
based almost exclusively on renewable sources of energy (wind, sun,
water, vegetable fuels) and materials (plant and animal products,
earth, glass, stone) but it is unusual to go this far. A less
extreme ecologically-based technology would be prepared to use any
technique that did not transgress a known "law" of ecological
balance (e.g. power from the wind, but stored as hydrogen generated
by electrolysis of water - a method requiring considerable technical
sophistication).

Resource Conserving Technology. This is strongly related to
ecological technology in that the flow of materials and energy are
inevitably ecological variables. Nevertheless there may be conflicts.
Increased use of biological materials in place of non-renewable
mineral resources may result in over-cropping and severe ecological
disruption. The two constraints together may result in an absolute
diminution of the flow of materials for production - a result which
some will applaud, but others will regard as very unfortunate if
it proves necessary. Some alternative technologies base themselves
on ethical principles about how resources should be apportioned,
in time as well as in space. This involves (implicitly) classifying
resources into various groups, and classifying the interested
parties into groups according to their "rights" as regards entitle-
ment to resources. This results in very deep differences, and different resource-disposing ground-rules for alternative technologies.
Most of these problems are resolved in a self-sufficient economy,
since there is negligible net in or outflow and no "using up".

Self-Sufficient Technology or Regional Technology. Ecological
and resource goals often point to local self-sufficiency as one
solution. There are social arguments also. Radical analyses of the
phenomenon of underdevelopment strongly emphasise the imbalance
between the "metropolis" and the "periphery", the centre exploiting
its client states. The same phenomenon is found in the metropolitan
countries themselves, where the cities exploit the countryside.
Meanwhile the cities themselves are sacrificed to the requirements
of international commerce. No area lives for itself, but for the

requirements of other parts of the system. Some have seen this as
the result of uneven accumulation of capital. Some of the reasons
for self-sufficiency can be summarised:

a) ecologically stable in that material is not depleted in
    one place and dispersed at another a great distance away
    as pollution;

b) the system does not exploit and cannot be exploited - at
    least not in a commercial sense;

c) the system does not depend on unreliable processes else-
    where in the system, and thus is more stable in the event
    of a general disturbance;

d) the economy can proceed at its own pace without having to
    compete with external economies;

e) if randomly selected, it would be a "worst case" - any
    collection of such units would probably be more efficient
    rather than less;

f) the population defines its goals in its own terms.

Very few AT enthusiasts take total self-sufficiency seriously,
but it is useful as a starting point. Nearly all decentralist
writings assume the presence of certain "seed" materials brought
in from outside of necessity. Sometimes just the principle is discussed and sometimes a specific size or even a specific region.
The Chinese case is well-known and without much doubt the most
successful ever attempted(1).

Self-Help Technology. This is a feature of nearly all alternative technologies, involving simplicity of production, use, maintenance,etc.(2); cheapness; and a certain independence of the
"normal economy", although much self-help technology uses scavenged
material which would simply not exist without the detritus of industry. Sometimes the idea is pressed to an individual level, but more
usually involves collective self-management. The break from normal
production techniques is motivated by the desire to regain direct
control over the production process, not to be "mystified" by

1) Jon Sigurdsson, "Rural Industrialisation in China", Science
    Policy Research Unit, University of Sussex, Brighton, England,
    1972.

2) Frances Stewart points out that these different simplicity
    requirements may conflict intrinsically (Study Group Background
    Paper No.11).

experts, and thus to take decisions "in full knowledge of the relevant facts" (Engels). Self-help technology fits well into a direct-democracy self-sufficient community, but has a much closer relationship to life in cities. Radicals see it as a means of raising consciousness by showing the possibilities for direct control, as in the case of squatters organising their own services such as plumbing and heating, or the running of small-scale "communal factories".

Revolutionary Technology. Many practitioners of alternative technologies feel them to be revolutionary in the negative sense that further developed, and under the appropriate circumstances, they could threaten the existing system by posing an alternative. Others have sought a more positive approach to attacking the existing order through unusual technical methods - e.g. "Computers for People", spreading information on how to block the operation of computer-systems. In between these two approaches is a compromise by those revolutionaries who feel that the orthodox type of revolution is no longer possible in industrial countries, and fall back on the idea of "islands" of revolutionary practice which can serve as bases for political activity. Near self-sufficiency would be desirable because of its security, and also as a means of testing out modes of production more in line with the revolutionary ideology.

Soft Technology (at last). In my conception, soft technology is a mixture of various elements of the alternative technologies discussed above. Such a mixture is only possible if there is not too much conflict between the means of achieving the various goals. However, most of the goals can be approached by stages, and to the extent that they conflict, the various parameters could be given weights in order to optimise overall. This is never done formally of course, but partisans of each desired goal try to make operational rules which could constitute minimum standards for creating "mixed" alternative technologies. The intuitive mix that I find in my subculture does not seem to find too much trouble reconciling the different demands, but that is mainly because there is much more theory than practice; and it is very easy to fool yourself. To take an example of conflicting demands the house recently designed, and soon to be built, by the BRAD group[1]. The heating system of the house is supposed to be ecologically sound, simple, and non resource-using, as far as possible. There is a solar wall

_____

1) Biotechnic Research and Development, 8 Lambert Street, London, N.1.

of a very simple type (good) which is also a structural member
(good), and made of "OK" materials (glass and concrete); but it
is not so efficient as a more sophisticated type of wall and supplementary heat is required; so a wood-burning stove is required
(good fuel, but more off-site material-iron); there is a limit to
the amount of fuel that can be cropped annually from the site, so
yet another source of heat is needed in the deep winter. Heat from
a stream is collected by a heat pump, which is technically rather
elaborate and manufactured off the site (bad), and requires power
from electricity off the site (bad), but much less than would be
needed for direct resistance heating (good). In constructing the
house, the use of polystyrene (bad) as an insulator would cut down
the need for electricity (good) but is also expensive (bad). Later
on, much of the operation of the heat pump can be taken over by a
windmill (good) which will require certain parts from off-site
(bad) ... and so on. The house is built slowly and carefully, and
is intended to last a very long time (good) but is costly (bad).
Another house currently under construction is being built very
cheaply and quickly, mostly from scavenged materials, just to show
what can be achieved by amateurs, and to "demystify" the process
of building: it is also intended to be relatively autonomous. It
is not supposed to be permanent: the materials can all be used
again. Which house is more "soft"?

So we could say that we are looking for techniques that would
be, let us say, not "inappropriate" to:

- the use of renewable or very abundant materials and sources
  of energy;
- remaining within the natural flow-rates;
- regional self-reliance for essentials;
- simplification in production and use;
- satisfaction in production and use;
- small-scale, self-managed production units.

Even if these various goals do not conflict with each other,
one great conflict remains: that between the goals and productivity.
Let us admit there would be fantastic losses in sheer productivity.
But there would also be gains. Nobody can say until it has been
tried, but such a system as alternative technologists and radical
economists propose would have at least some claim to rationality,
because:

a) "residual" factors would be released (as in China)(1);

b) in rational production for local needs there would be no superfluous production; neither would there be useless jobs;

c) diminution of leisure-time consumption would be compensated by the enjoyment of work;

d) there would be no waste through exploitation or uneven accumulation of capital;

e) apparent sacrifices of opportunities in the upper reaches of utility curves is not great: within limits, the frugality game can be just as rewarding as the opulence game;

f) "non-economic" satisfactions would be attacked directly, rather than indirectly through the medium of exchange.

Goodness what a lot of special pleading!

Alternative Science. This is at the other end of alternative technology from alternative society, and it is always hard to tell where one begins and the other ends. As with "alternative technology", "alternative science" tends to refer not so much to truly original or unknown things, but to means of organising knowledge. There are a number of formal suggestions, such as an alliance of scientists and those whose interests are not normally served by the scientific establishment or the government; the organisation of science on a community basis serving local needs. Informally, the idea that much of our knowledge is not teachable but only learnable through direct experience is growing strongly. Such non-academic trends are starting to cross-fertilise with some tendencies within the academy, such as the resurgence of interest in the sociology of knowledge and the status of scientific objectivity. There might not be such a gulf between Polanyi and Mao.

Soft technology is not for export. If the people of the Third World want televisions and motor-cars, that is fine. It may well be that the somewhat paradoxical Intermediate Technology claim is correct - that by not going for the really big technology too hastily in the first instance, balanced growth occurs faster and

---

1) Jack Gray's article "The Chinese Model; Some Characteristics of Maoist Policies for Social Change and Economic Growth" in Socialist Economics, Ed. Alec Nove and D.M. Nuti (Penguin, 1972) makes much of the major originality of Maoist economic policy, not in deploying the available resources, but in releasing hidden resources.

the capacity to mass-produce consumer goods is achieved sooner.
It may also be the case that maximising GNP growth is not the
most rational way of achieving development goals (even to the
extent that GNP growth rate may rate as an inverse measure of
social justice). But this is none of our business, technologically.
The task of the citizen in the industrial countries who wishes to
help the Third World is here in the belly of the beast, actively
opposing the dominance of the "centre" over the periphery. Some
of us at least see soft technology and its associated ideology
serving, however humbly, that purpose.

This is all a bit half-baked of course. Fortunately nobody
minds that too much in the movement, although I am embarrassed to
be writing it here. I would appreciate any feedback from other
subcultures.

2. Denis Goulet:

a) Value Problems in the Choice and Adaptation of Technology

My basic assumption is that all change ought to be as harmon-
ious as possible with any society's cherished values so as to minimise its human costs and to foster participation by the people in
development decisions and their implementation. Here I address the
key question: "Who are the actors or agents of change?" The standard answer is that planners, experts, or change catalysts are the
main agents or actors. But there is an opposite view, to which
Max Millikan alluded in 1962 when he wrote:

> "the process of arriving at a national plan should be one
> in which the planners present to the community for discussion
> a variety of critical choices showing for each alternative
> the consequences for the society of pursuing that value choice
> consistently and efficiently. It is only by this process that
> the community can clarify its individual and social goals"(1).

If this is the case for national planning (by definition a
macro arena of choices) a fortiori does it hold also for national

---

1) Max F. Millikan, "Criteria for Decision-Making in Economic
   Planning - The Planning Process and Planning Objectives in
   Developing Countries", in Organisation, Planning and Programming for Economic Development, Vol. VIII of the U.S. papers
   prepared for the UN Conference on the Application of Science
   and Technology for the Benefit of the Less Developed Areas,
   U.S. Government Printing Office, 1962, pp.28-38.

technology policy (likewise a macro arena) and local technology choices (a micro arena)? I think that Millikan is too optimistic regarding planners' ability to map out "alternative consequences for the society of pursuing that value choice." Planners are as ignorant of these consequences as the populace itself. Only permanent, critical dialogue with people can lead to a realistic estimate of alternative value costs. The veritable "actors" are the experts or planners acting together with the interested populace.

What are the main "factors" of successful adaptation? The main factor, in my view, is the image of change both sets of "actors" have as they plan. Hirschman has shown that one's image of change is itself a decisive factor affecting change(1). Therefore, experts and planners must have a correct image of a society's value structure and its capacity for technological change. Too often, however, experts view "backward" societies as stagnant, unreceptive to change, indifferent to efficiency, hostile to modern technology or to problem-solving rationality. This view is erroneous and constitutes an obstacle to the successful adoption of technological change at the grass-roots level.

Most societies possess an existence rationality which is highly receptive to change. Existence rationality is simply the strategy any society adopts to achieve life-sustenance, esteem, and freedom (as it defines these values) within two systems of constraints:

- its information-processing capacities; and
- the effective access it enjoys to resources.

Any existence rationality contains certain core values, relating to minimum requirements for survival, freedom, and esteem as well as outer boundaries of secondary values, where great flexibility is possible.

What is the practical implication of this analysis? Change can best occur when outside change catalysts, in conjunction with the populace itself, restructure the outer boundaries of the society's existence rationality. Core values must not be directly challenged, since these values protect a society's optimum performance in meeting its demands for survival, identify, and freedom. Good change strategies will operate at the boundaries by altering the range of possibilities. This is done in two ways:

---

1) See Albert O. Hirschman, The Strategy of Economic Development, Yale University Press, 1965, pp.11-20.

- by increasing the society's capacity to process information
  (not merely increasing its stock of information); and

- increasing the resources to which the society in question
  has effective access. The key word here is effective(1).

Three obstacles stand in the way of successful adaptation of
technology in most situations of "under-development":

a) long before the information-processing capacities of a
   society are increased, its desire mechanisms are transformed by demonstration effects and symbolic impingements
   of many kinds. The lid is blown off the constraints on
   desire;

b) even when information-processing capacity (and not merely
   information) increases, effective access to resources
   usually remains closed to most members of society;

c) finally, long after greater resources become available
   they can be obtained, in most cases, only on commercial
   terms which discriminate against those whose needs are
   greatest because their purchasing power is lower.

When these three tensions operate jointly, they account for
most of the value conflicts in technology transfers at the local
level. One also finds their parallel at the national level, in
technology exchanges from "developed" to "under-developed" countries.

I believe that the work of such people as Robert Caillot and
Helmut Krauch must be enriched by rigorous studies to evaluate
results obtained when their approach is applied to specific problems of choosing appropriate technologies. The basic principle
shared by Caillot and Krauch is a commitment to consult the populace itself, at all stages of decision-making, regarding the direction, the speed and the nature of changes to be adopted; both in-
sist on the need to widen the informational horizons of the populace by suitable macro-information about economics, demography,
infra-structure networks, and the like. According to both, better
decisions about efficiency and cost benefit are obtained when
"experts" first submit their alternative decisions to a popular

---

1) A fuller explanation of the notion of existence rationality
   is given in Denis Goulet's, The Cruel Choice, A New Concept
   in the Theory of Development, Atheneum, 1971, pp. 188-212,
   (Paperback edition available since 1973).

debate conducted in a setting of reciprocity. Krauch's use of computer consoles in his consultations has two advantages: it initiates the populace itself to an important tool of modern technology, and it makes possible consultation with large numbers of people(1).

Another suggestion I wish to make is to undertake a study to see how populations of different sizes, degrees of homogeneity, and levels of technological sophistication themselves choose and adapt their technologies. Do they select more appropriate technologies than those recommended by "experts"? Are their choices consonant with national development goals, with the demands of efficiency, of economy, etc? How does the populace at large judge the merits of macro-technologies which must be adopted by units larger than those which they themselves can control, or even understand?

The main objective in all this is to improve methods whereby suitable choices of a whole range of technologies can be made. Much progress in this direction has already been achieved by the Andian Pact countries in their dealing with exports of technology.

b) <u>Costs and Commercialisation of Technology Transfer</u>

Spokesmen for multi-national corporations (e.g. José R.Bejarano, Vice President of Xerox) usually allege that technologies required for successful development in Third World nations are too expensive for governments to provide to their countries by their own effort. Consequently, they conclude that underdeveloped countries should simply accept transfers of technology from multi-national corporations on commercial terms.

Indeed, as Mr. Sabato has explained, technology does in fact operate as a privileged commodity, which penetrates underdeveloped countries without tariffs. Mr. Giral and others have suggested that underdeveloped countries should simply accept the commercial ground rules governing technological exchanges and strive to improve their bargaining position so as to negotiate more successfully with suppliers of technology. This view, however, raised the larger problem of structural dependency in transfers.

---

1) Caillot has described his work in "L'Enquête-Participation à L'Economie et Humanisme" in <u>Cahiers de l'Institut Canadien d'Education des Adultes</u>, No.3 (Feb.1967), pp.121-144, and in "Une Connaissance Engagée: L'Enquête-Participation" in <u>Options Humanistes</u>, (Paris: Les Editions Ouvrières, 1968), pp.55-80. Helmut Krauch, papers delivered at C.S.D.I. (Santa Barbara, California). "Experiments, Experience and Planning", "Public Control of Government Planning" "Can Reality be Simulated?"

Several members of the work group have evoked the larger ambitions of underdeveloped countries. It is not enough for them to buy patents, obtain licenses, or even receive the advice of consultants on a commercial basis. Underdeveloped countries must, in general terms, gain open access to scientific and technological information.

The premise here is that the capacity of a country to sustain technological innovation is the major resource of relevance to development efforts today, of greater importance than natural resources or of capital. Therefore the crucial question is not to choose or adapt suitable technologies, but to devise appropriate channels through which access to the pool of scientific and technological knowledge can be assured to underdeveloped countries on other than commercial terms.

It is precisely these commercial ground rules which protect the favoured position of multi-national firms and of developed countries vis-à-vis underdeveloped countries and units within the latter: firms, specific agencies, universities. This international division of labour is one of the main instruments whereby development efforts in poorer countries can be domesticated.

This means, in short, that overall strategy must do two things:

- identify precise working points at which leverage for greater bargaining position in negotiations can be increased for underdeveloped countries and units therein; and

- begin pressuring the international economic order in the direction of eventually creating a world-wide technological pool. The aim here, ultimately, is to remove scientific and technological information and arts from the realm of commercialisation.

3. J. de Bandt

A. Technology and Factor Costs. Before choosing a technology, the decision-maker must first select his reference criteria. In considering how far technology is adapted to the quantity and quality of available factors, it is important to reflect upon the criteria for assessing that adaptation, particularly the relative factor costs.

From the development point of view, technology should be adapted in the light of relative prices only when those prices actually reflect the availability of factors and on the supplementary condition that account is taken not only of the immediate data concerning availability but also of data on availability in the future (or alternative assumptions about the future).

Influenced by capital aid, relative prices do in fact bias the choice of technology in the direction of capital intensification thereby quite considerably reducing the volume of employment for any given output.

This bias in the choice of technology is all the more ominous in that the capital cost of delivered goods in developing countries is appreciably higher, with the result that investment in developing countries involves higher capital ratios than in the developed countries.

This higher capital cost stems not only from transfer costs, but in many cases from the fact that the investment involves an intra-corporate operation.

This is explained by the fact that the investment benefits from low-interest loans and the capital equipment is delivered in kind to developing countries. The profitability of the operation for the private promotor is assured, to a varying extent, by the difference between the nominal invoiced value of this equipment and the true purchase cost. The same situation applies to the acquisition of replacement parts.

This sort of situation calls for two kinds of measures:

- in the matter of capital cost, it is essential as a minimum that capital operations should not be based on public loans.

- in the matter of relative prices, it is essential that present financial criteria be abandoned as a base for capital aid, which should be tendered as an aid to employment.

B. <u>Technical Information</u>. Technical information raises problems not only of availability (access to information) and compilation (collection, organisation, distribution), but perhaps even more important, of content, and more particularly how far it covers the whole range of existing technical possibilities.

In fact, taking into account the origin of technical information and the reasons for which it is disseminated, it most often covers a limited area of technical possibilities. So, according to the nature of those limits, the choice of technology is distorted from the outset.

Concrete examples can be given concerning information on the type of equipment needed in the textiles industry to satisfy certain requirements of product quality, safe working and competition. The most notorious example of the latter is information designed to impose the idea that the textile production processes have become markedly capital intensive and can therefore function competitively only by using sophisticated equipment.

4. J. Perrin

"Engineering" and the Control of Technology

The expression "engineering" is used here in its American usage - the design of investment projects and the management of their implementation. Engineering is also a profession which is exercised partly or wholly by different types of organisation: consulting engineers, engineering contractors.

The autonomy of "engineering" is relatively new in the industrialisation process. It is linked to the importance of information in the second industrial revolution. As a result of the development of mechanisation and automation in modern industry (especially continuous process industries) scientific and technical information becomes more important in the design phase than in the production phase.

Engineering, because of its role in the design and implementation of projects, must establish close relations with other industrial activities: R and D, production, capital equipment supply. But these are not unidirectional: they are dialectical, especially in the case of the link with capital equipment production.

Developed country engineering organisations which take part in LDC investment projects have their own logic: to promote the sale of equipment from their country of origin. These firms necessarily have a tendance to promote turnkey sales in export markets. Others have observed that these developed country engineering organisations, as a result of their activities in developing countries, accumulate experience and knowledge which is fed back into their own industrial systems. There is thus a transfer in the wrong direction.

To transfer technologies or rather to control technology, LDCs must create their own engineering organisations. Association agreement with experienced engineering organisations can be used for this. But the experiences already attempted in this field show the difficulties and dangers of such agreements.

The concrete proposals for the Development Centre's programme may be suggested:

- Analysis of the movement in the share of turnkey projects

in total investment as a measure of LDCs control of technologies;

- Assembly and analysis of association agreements between LDC and DC engineering organisations.

5. H. Havemann: Need for Technology Aid

The discussions have covered a very wide field and many aspects of "Transfer and Choice of Technology". To come to conclusions concerning measures to be taken I suggest that we differentiate between types of technology:

i) Industrial technology: technologies adapted to the production of commercial goods; they must be adapted to different degrees - from slight alterations to major modifications.

ii) Innovative technology: new or very much modified conventional technology to achieve adjustments to conditions in developing countries: materials, forms of energy, etc.

iii) Advanced technology: almost unadaptable technology such as nuclear or space-engineering, etc. which is practically unalterable and transferred without changes to developing countries.

Roughly according to these groupings, measures should be conceived for choice and adaptation, as well as the transfer process. Thus, the first category of technology calls for an interaction mainly between companies. The second category is to be evolved by research and development mainly, and thus concerns governments or private enterprise mainly and research organisations. The third, finally, is a matter for government institutions alone.

To arrive at a profile of the needs of a less developed country, a new type of "country programme" should be evolved which assesses the situation of a country and analyses it as to needs and possibilities of science and technology. This would result in a decision as to which categories of technology should be applied - as also the details within each category. This would constitute "country planning for science and technology".

For this, recourse should be taken to international co-operation - to its bilateral as well as multilateral forms. It is strongly suggested to conceive for this purpose, of a new form of development aid, i.e. technology aid. The reason for this suggestion is the conviction, created particularly by the discussions of the Study Group, that technology as applied to development is too complex to be handled by the usual and conventional instruments of development and practised up to now. Correspondingly, institutions should be established in developed as well as developing countries to carry this new "technology aid" whereby an international coordination could be achieved, e.g. by UNIDO.

Following my previous remarks I want to make two more points:

i) "choice of technology" has also to take into account the international division of labour, i.e. industrial production. This has to be directed in such a way that international exchanges of goods can be established in a concerted way. This undoubtedly affects the choice of technology to be introduced into the developing country. Admittedly, this is both a complex, as also a very long range, consideration, but nevertheless it has to be kept in mind.

ii) "Research and Development" has been mentioned in the context of "Choice of technology" but in my opinion not with the emphasis it actually commands. Mr. Stepanek pointed to the need to take it more seriously in future. I fully agree, but suggest that this is a special aspect of the previously suggested technology aid, i.e. its innovative, original aspect. We can, for its realisation, think of universities, e.g. the "International University System" of the United Nations, or also of other organisational forms. But appropriate technology without the element of innovation seems to me to be an incomplete conception.

6. P.C. Trussell: Some Reflections.

On the definition of terms (appropriate, intermediate, convenient - technology), I consider this whole business academic, and I would suggest picking the least offensive terms and sticking to them. Having spent 2-3 hours, at a cost of about $2,500 per hour, too much has already been expended.

On the economic side of "appropriate" technology, I think that de Bandt's point was well taken not to go overboard for labour intensiveness for processes and products as the economics may be soft; the selection on the basis of low capital intensity may in many cases be economic, but not necessarily in all. The big consideration is whether the marketed product is for the domestic or foreign trade.

I rather feel there is an over-emphasis on the licensing of new sophisticated inventions; most of the manufacture done in the world uses either non-patented processes or processes on which patents have run out.

A most important aspect and one that has received no direct attention at this meeting is making assistance available at the bottom level in backward societies. All societies have latent entrepreneurs - the problem is finding them and giving them a chance for expression (entrepreneurs almost never come from the university-trained segment of society). One of the more effective ways of meeting this problem I am aware of, is that being carried out by the Pan-American Development Foundation (office at Washington D.C.) by making low-interest rate loans to people on the bottom floor in the economy, to finance designated projects of small groups or cooperatives. These loans are made through banks, not by governments without the usual requirement of collateral. Pay-backs have normally run over 90 per cent. This work is well worth investigating. It is strictly action operation.

I must heartily subscribe to Sabato's statement that R and D and Technical Information and Know-how are marketable commodities, and our concern should be to see that the developing countries get a fair deal on anything they pay for.

Implementation of technological developments in LDCs will be a difficult matter (as it is in advanced countries as any inventor or conceptual R and D man will confirm). There are many ways of meeting this problem, and the means used will depend on the specific case and the specific market environment. One of the big hurdles that has not been mentioned is high interest rates in many LDCs which makes risk capital for new ventures very difficult to obtain.

Part Three

SUMMARIES OF BACKGROUND PAPERS

I. INTERMEDIATE TECHNOLOGY AND RELATED SUBJECTS

INTERMEDIATE TECHNOLOGY : A DEFINITIONAL DISCUSSION
(Background Paper No.11)

by

Frances Stewart
(Excerpts)

The first part of this paper provides an extensive discussion
of some of the characteristics of IT that have been suggested as
essential aspects. They are:

a) low capital cost per work place;
b) low capital cost per unit of output;
c) low capital cost per machine;
d) simplicity:

 i) manufacture;
 ii) in operation;
 iii) maintenance and repair;
 iv) organisation

e) non-modern sector;
f) rural-sector;
g) small-scale;
h) use of local inputs;
i) self-help.

Some of the ambiguities and difficulties are discussed(1).
Some techniques fulfil some of the characteristics but **not** others.
On the basis of that discussion the second part of the paper discusses those characteristics which will be the particular concern
of this research.

---

1) Part of the discussion is cited in Part One, Chapter I of this
report.

a) K/L: The employment and poverty problem of developing
countries can be regarded as primarily caused by two factors;
first, the absolute shortage of complementary factors, particularly
capital; and secondly, the disproportion in the way these factors
are applied. Flexible factor proportions in one sector (the traditional) and rigid factor proportions in the other (the modern)
leads to great disparities in rates of capital formation per head,
productivity and incomes per head, and consequent dissatisfaction
with employment opportunities in the traditional sector. The technology required may therefore either be a modern sector technology
with lower K/L than 'Western' technology, and/or a traditional
sector technology involving higher rates of capital per man than
current techniques. The intermediate nature of the technology is
thus clear. It can be defined as low K/L technology, though this
is relative to the current technology in the modern sector.

It has often been argued that techniques of low K/L involve
lower savings rates and therefore lower rates of growth in output
and employment. The argument depends on uniformity of wages irrespective of technique, particular assumptions about savings behaviour out of profits, and government inability to enforce the savings rate it desires. The argument is not accepted here as justi-
fication for choosing high K/L techniques.

b) K/O: As there is a direct link between output and technique it is unusual for output to be homogeneous with two different techniques. Hence a weighting system is required which presents
difficulties because of income distribution. But assuming that these
problems - and the more difficult ones of capital measurement - are
satisfactorily solved, techniques which require higher capital/
output ratios will mean lower levels of output, income and probably
savings. In general, therefore, techniques which raise K/O ratios
should not be chosen though care must be taken with measurement of
the ratios, particularly where each technique involves different
income distribution, as they very often do.

c) Cost per machine: This is connected with the scale question - (g). The requirement for low capital cost per machine is
conditional on the requirement that the technique is applicable
on a small scale, and is therefore divisible.

d) Simplicity: Simplicity of manufacture is only a requirement if local manufacture is desired. Simplicity of operation is
in general a requirement if the attempt to economise on scarce
capital resources is not to be offset by using scarce labour
resources. Simplicity of repair and maintenance is of greater

importance for small scale operation than for large scale, where
skilled repair and maintenance can be maintained.

e) <u>Non-modern sector</u>: The employment problem may be tackled
by reducing capital intensity in the modern sector or by increasing
that in the traditional sector. The relative numbers in both sectors suggests that in many countries concentration on modifying
techniques adopted in the modern sector will have little impact
on the main problem of labour under-utilisation for many years.
It appears that the only way of affecting the majority of people
is to provide improved techniques in the traditional sector. Nomenclature is largely a matter of taste; the use of the terms ('non-
modern' or 'traditional') to describe the application of changed
technology to the traditional sector is possibly useful to indicate
that it is a question of raising technology, capital per head, and
productivity in the traditional sector rather than changing modern
sector technology. There is also the question of modifying technology in the modern sector in a labour intensive way.

f) <u>Rural</u>: The non-modern sector extends to urban as well as
rural areas, though probably the majority of those in the traditional sector are in the rural areas. I would therefore prefer to drop
the rural/urban distinction as a defining characteristic of the
required technology, though the appropriate technology might well
prove to be different in the town and country, and not only because
products differ, but because markets, tastes, factor incomes and
transport costs do also.

g) <u>Small-scale</u>: The small-scale requirement makes the technology available to those with access to limited amounts of capital,
and who have never or only in a small way operated as entrepreneurs
before. It is connected with the non-modern sector requirement,
since modern Western technology sector tends to be relatively large-
scale, and introduction of new technology to the traditional sector
must initially at least be on a small scale.

h) <u>Local inputs</u>: This requirement is connected with the desire
to stimulate linkage effects of the technology. It is also probably
a good way of getting new techniques off the ground in the traditional sector.

i) <u>Self-help</u>: This requirement, which presumably means that
those who use the technique are not too dependent on outside (especially foreign) sources for i) finance; and ii) technology, in terms
of machinery, operation and maintenance, is more likely to be fulfilled the more small scale are the operations, and where the simplicity requirement is fulfilled.

The self-help characteristic differs from the others discussed as being an end in itself, whereas the others are means to ends. Some are means to means - e.g. low capital cost per machine is a means to the possibility of small-scale production, itself a means to non-traditional non-modern activities, and to self-help.

There is one broad distinction which emerges from this discussion: between the modern and non-modern sector. Technology appropriate for the non-modern sector has to be suitable for small-scale operation, and therefore each machine must be cheap, simple to operate and maintain. Technology appropriate for the modern sector needs to be more labour-intensive than current Western technology, but may otherwise be similar in kind - large-scale, etc. The question of product - type and quality - has been ignored up to now. In the traditional sector the new technology will be as much a question of developing new products - of extending the range of products, as of adopting different techniques of production to produce the same type of output.

CHOICE AND ADAPTATION OF TECHNOLOGY IN DEVELOPING COUNTRIES
(INDIAN EXPERIENCE)
(Background Paper No. 38)

by

K. L. Nanjappa
(Abstract)

The appropriateness of a technology to be adopted cannot emerge out of an exercise deliberately undertaken with some preconceived idea; rather, it is the knowledge, experience, hereditary skills, the requirements of the trade, the suitability of raw materials for being processed by an appropriate system of technology, etc., which will enable an entrepreneur to decide for himself the technology he should adopt. Indian experience is a proof of this.

The Industrial Policy Resolutions of 1948 and 1956 recognised the importance and desirability of large factories and of small industries, on the one hand, and the cottage units managed by families, on the other.

This thinking is reflected in the successive Five-Year Economic Development Plans. For example, the Common Production Programme, adopted in the field of certain industries during the Second Five-Year Plan, recognised that technology apart, the scale of operations could be another guiding factor in demarcating the lines of production for the large and small industries sector in the country.

In 1954, an International Team on Small Scale Industries set up by the Ford Foundation, studied the opportunities of increasing both industrial production and employment in two major groups of industries:

 i) traditional village craftsmen (carpenters, blacksmiths, potters, etc.) working mainly within their village and occasionally for the nearby communities;

 ii) small industries aiming at larger markets (all the country and abroad).

In the first group, the team found that the introduction of new and sophisticated technologies should aim at increased productivity and this would necessarily require the artisans active participation.

In the second group, the Ford Foundation Team suggested establishment of Multipurpose Institutes of Technology for Small Scale Industries, intended to:

 i) initiate and carry out investigations and surveys to promote the development of small industry;

 ii) disseminate the results thus obtained to the existing or potential industrialists or organisations.

In other words, the basic tasks were: to promote the use of quality materials, more efficient tools, better machinery, methods and design; to promote better marketing, both by the study of the demand and by the organisation of marketing channels; to conduct surveys and a market news service; to study and improve the credit facilities, the management capabilities, etc.

The task of the Institutes to disseminate the results obtained should be performed as follows:

 i) through education at the regional institutes, at the branch units or offices, through other transmission channels (trade associations, cooperatives, community projects, etc.);

ii) through information and consultation services (instructors, branch offices, industrial extension workers, mobile demonstration units, etc.);

iii) through the establishment of a publications service, libraries, exhibitions and other media.

The concept which guided the Ford Foundation Team was rather the "need-based" than the appropriate or intermediate technology concept.

Established in 1954, following the recommendations made by the Ford Foundation team, the Small Scale Industries Development Organisation (SSIDO) performs two main functions:

- the study of the evolvement of the technical schemes, the training and demonstration of the improved methods of production, the guidance and knowledge about the process of manufacture, etc.;

- the work of the Technical Extension Service.

The SSIDO tries to adapt the real experience gained in developed countries (Japan, West Germany, UK, France, USA, etc.) and organises study tours for its officials and for industrialists in these countries.

SSIDOs Survey Teams, which include economists, technicians, cost accountants, etc., define model schemes of particular product lines in the given situation of the country, and thus evolve a need-based technology for each case. To quote a few examples, special model schemes have been established for the production of such goods as boot polish, leather goods and footwear, preserved fruits, woollen hosiery, electric motors, paints and varnishes, etc. Thus, the small scale industry sector in India embraces today a whole range from elementary blacksmith and carpentry units to the most sophisticated ones using automatic machinery.

The dissemination of the new need-based technologies plays an important part in SSIDOs work: mobile vans equipped with improved yet simple types of machinery in carpentry, wood working, ceramics-pottery, etc., complete the work of the system of extension centres and workshops existing throughout the country. SSIDO thinks that seeing is believing and believing is the beginning of action.

Initially, SSIDO had Regional Offices located in Calcutta, Bombay, New Delhi and Madras but it has been decentralised and, at present, each State has a Major Institute and, in certain States, there are branches of the Major Institutes. These Institutes identify and define the model schemes and the need-based technologies, organise the training of the personnel on the improved machinery, test the quality of the products being manufactured by the small-scale units, and develop the product/processes of a large number of items.

So far, the Organisation has prepared model schemes on 247 products, impact schemes on 234 products, feasibility reports on 9 products, industrial outlook survey reports on 150 items, industries prospect sheets on 304 products, all of them dealing directly with the concept of appropriate technology.

A special effort has been made in favour of the rural and backward areas, by preparing special schemes for the entrepreneurs who want to set up industries in this sector and by designing and developing the machinery and equipment adapted to the degree of skills available in these regions.

To conclude, we can say that SSIDO has faced many difficulties (lack of the technical know-how to identify the appropriate technology, unavailability of the right type of machinery, etc.) but with the help of international organisations (UNIDO, APO, ILO, UNDP, Ford Foundation, etc.) these difficulties have been solved to some extent.

The technology is not always the most modern one, but the Council of Scientific and Industrial Research and the National Committee on Science and Technology make a great effort to evolve the need-based technologies for the industry.

Efforts are also being made to establish a close liaison between the large and small units by way of ancillaries so that the latter gets the benefit of the knowledge and experience of the large units in adopting modern techniques for making the final end-product.

The small-scale industries sector has provided large opportunities of gainful employment to the population of the country and managed to satisfy the consumer with products whose quality is good and prices not higher than in the large-scale industrial sector.

GENESIS, ORGANISATION AND ACTION PROGRAMME OF
THE APPROPRIATE TECHNOLOGY CELL
(Background Paper No. 1)

by

Bepin Behari
(Summary)

The Indian authorities had for long accepted the idea that
technology must be adapted to the particular conditions (of all
kinds) in the country in which it has to be applied, this idea
being connected with the philosophy of Mahatma Gandhi on the
reciprocal influences of a civilisation and the technological
progress which it can absorb. The idea found a particularly favour-
able climate due to the considerable importance which the Planning
Commission had attached, from its inception, to small industry and
rural industry (projects for industrialising rural areas and pilot
experiments in 49 areas throughout the country).

For this reason, the Ministry of Industrial Development set
up in 1969 an Inderdepartmental Committee under the chairmanship
of the Secretary of State, Shri K. Balachandram, to work out what
practical measures to take. Its first reports at once highlighted
the complexity and interdisciplinarity of the problems raised and
came to the conclusion that a special co-ordinating unit would
have to be set up to carry out socio-economic studies, identify
technical problems, design technological prototypes in liaison
with various laboratories and technological research establishments,
direct pilot experiments in order to test their viability and,
lastly, assemble and distribute the appropriate documentation and
data.

These are the terms of reference of the new unit, called
"Appropriate Technology Cell", which has been set up in the Ministry
of Industrial Development in liaison with the Planning Commission
on the understanding that its functions would include "negotiating
with private industry on exploiting the processes deemed acceptable".

Rather than study particular types of machinery, the Appropriate Technology Cell has concentrated on three aspects of production programming, viz:

a) product design,
b) manufacturing techniques and
c) organisation and management of production units.

The main factors in choosing technologies are the scale of operations, the factor costs, the natural assets of the place in question as regards resources and skills, and a whole list of other qualitative variations in the factors of production which might affect the efficiency of a given technology. In addition to all these requirements on the production side, there are the requirements on the consumption side, the constraints of standard specifications and the tolerance limits, as well as all the social and economic data concerning the industry in question.

In view of the part they play in the national economy and of their impact on employment, on the standard of life of the rural population (including their deterrent effect on the rural exodus) and on the use of local raw materials and transport facilities, special priority has been given to the following sectors:

a) <u>Traditional crafts in rural areas</u>

  Pottery, iron-working, joinery, gold-working, weaving, etc.

b) <u>Small village industries</u> of the kind dealt with by the Khadi and Village industries Commission:

  1. Khadi (cottage spinning).
  2. Processing of cereals and pulses.
  3. Village oil-presses.
  4. Village leather-working.
  5. Cottage match manufacture.
  6. Gur and khandsari (unrefined sugar) manufacture.
  7. Palm gur sugar manufacture.
  8. Production of inedible oils and soap.
  9. Paper-making by hand.
  10. Bee-keeping.
  11. Village potteries.
  12. Treatment of vegetable fibres.
  13. Joinery and blacksmith industry.
  14. Lime-making.

15. Making gobar gas (methane).
16. Aluminium-working.
17. Wood-working.
18. Fruit preserving.
19. Katha-processing (a bark used for making dyes).
20. Making articles of vickers and bamboo.

c) Industries based on agriculture

i) Food industries

Preservation of vegetables and fruits, dairy industry, gur and khandsari industry, production of cattle-feed, production of poultry-feed, production of powdered egg, production of pork foods, fish preserves, bee-keeping, and shark's liver products.

ii) Textile industries

Textiles and vegetable fibre industries, hosiery, coconut fibre spinning, making surgical cotton, and ginning and treating cotton.

iii) Firewood and wood-working industries

Sawmilling and wood-drying, furniture-making, making accessories for hand-looms, making tools and instruments, and making wooden toys, shoe-trees and clothes hangers.

iv) Industries supplying products for use in agriculture

Manufacture of electric motors, diesel engines, agricultural appliances, pumps, and equipment for poultry-breeding, milk-processing, fishing and forestry, manufacture of plant for producing methane from dung, manufacture of pesticides.

v) Miscellaneous industries

Manufacture of bricks and tiles, together with their associated industries, manufacture of bone fertiliser, leather industry, rubber manufactures.

An intensive study is also being made of the following six sectors:

1. Tanning and the manufacture of footwear and leather goods.

2. The ceramics industry (including pottery a

3. The food industry and fruit-preserving.

4. The manufacture of agricultural implements.

5. Operating large-scale processes on a smaller scale, especially oil-refining, cement-making and paper-making.

6. Building and road making.

The funds and staff available to the Appropriate Technology Cell for carrying out this ambitious programme are extremely limited, but it is agreed that the Cell is to act mainly as a source of inspiration and a co-ordinating centre which will delegate its authority and "sub-contract" its operational and research work to the many specialised Indian organisations, the starting point for each line of enquiry always being provided by the work done by a largely multi-disciplinary and versatile Working Party.

INTERMEDIATE TECHNOLOGIES FOR TRUE DEVELOPMENT
(Background Paper No.16)

by

A. Latham-Koenig

(Abstract)

To cope with mass unemployment (25-30 per cent according to ILO) and explosive city growth in LDCs, the mass production techniques of the West, which are labour-saving and capital intensive, are not appropriate: they exacerbate the problems of the dual society and rural/urban imbalance, they eliminate traditional activities, they put the poor country in a position of dependence on the righ aid givers, and, above all, they fail to create the jobs essential for rapidly growing populations.

The average equipment cost per work place of modern industry is of the order of £1,500 - £2,000. If we consider technology not as a given factor but as an important variable element, which can and should be adapted to the LDCs conditions, then we reach the concept of "intermediate" technologies. These technologies are essentially applied in rural areas with local resources, local skills and even locally made tools. The task is, as Gandhi put it, to generate not mass production but production by the masses. It

e 20 men each at a £100 work place, than

ιg a £2,000 piece of equipment even if the

e than the former.

industries in the rural areas would include:
ιgricultural inputs, the processing and stor-
etal fabrication and wood-working, building

ommunication gap, detailed information about
aₚₚ   gies needs to be collected, subjected to field
trials and ц   ₃d in suitable forms for communication to LDCs.

The ITDG Group, founded in 1965, is a small pragmatic and
action-oriented body. Each subject is tackled by multi-disciplinary
panels comprising engineers, scientists, architects, economists,
etc., and close links have been established with industry, technological institutions and universities.

Examples of successful achievements could be mentioned: the
construction of a hand operated multi-purpose metal bending machine
by the Agricultural Panel, the development of low cost methods of
conserving sparse water supplies by the Water Panel, the preparation
of industrial profiles, etc.

PARTICIPATION AND TECHNOLOGY DEVELOPMENT POLICIES:
NOTES ON PROBLEMS IN AFRICA

(Background Paper No.31)

by

Roland Colin

(Summary)

There are two reasons why the technological basis of any
development policy is important. First, one cannot raise the standard of living without improving technology; and secondly, the
developing countries cannot achieve real independence unless their
technology is improved.

In Africa, technological progress began with the colonial era,
but the colonial powers only transferred technology to Africa in
so far as it suited them to do so, which is why neolithic or iron-
age techniques still survived during that period, while on the

other hand the motor vehicle wheel was introduced into Africa before animal-drawn wheeled vehicles had been fully developed.

Until African countries became independent, their external sector, which was linked with the mother country, made use of the technology of the industrialised world (in transport, communications, etc.), while their traditional sector was handicapped by conservatism or technological decline, often concealed behind a policy of popular education. The traditional sector was run by the modernised sector by exerting administrative or educational (rural counselling) pressure on it.

Ten years after independence the situation is still unchanged, except that the Anglo-Saxon countries have evolved the "intermediate technology" approach as part of the self-help and community development system, which can be fitted into traditional structures and at the same time lead to improved living conditions by setting up small units working with traditional tools, local raw materials and skills, etc.

Although this system may be regarded as designed to provide "safety valves" without undermining the developed countries' overall control, it is nevertheless capable of producing an immediate improvement in the living standards of the populations concerned.

One might ask whether "intermediate technology" could not go further and even change the relationship between social forces. China is interesting in that respect, since it has achieved great progress at little human "cost". The Chinese took the countryside, as much as the towns, as their starting point for technological development by creating poles of technological growth in it. An important stage in this policy was to split up complex technological sequences into elementary steps so as to make them easier for the peasants to master. The policy was supported by the provision of explanations, information and training. It encouraged the peasants to be inventive and creative and led to revolutionary results (e.g. peasants who started by being illiterate ended by running the technical side of a transistor factory).

Can African countries follow the Chinese example? They remain closely attached to their former mother countries, especially as regards education. If the French speaking countries are to follow the example of the English speaking countries which have adopted the "intermediate technology" approach, one must first collect information on the latter, and this might be done by setting up, with the help of suitable international co-operation, one or more "intermediate technology data banks". In some respects this would coincide with the policy followed by UNIDO, although one does not find that Organisation producing the major results which would seem possible. For while it is fairly easy to solve the problem of collecting and processing technological data, we seem to be still far from having a satisfactory system for studying how to disseminate it and studying the environmental data and the necessary forms of training to be given.

Technology has to be adapted to African conditions and the socio-cultural system in Africa has to be made capable of mastering technological innovation, which brings us to the problem of "participation". This is to be achieved by making innovations understood and linking them with the particular social objectives of the community thanks to an educational effort based on internal conditions rather than on models outside the developing countries.

In Senegal a team from the IRFED is working with Senagalese officials, under the _sole_ control of the Senegalese Government, on a pilot experiment for training young people to pursue the development of rural technology in partnership with the peasant communities working with government instructors.

This experiment is epoch-making in Africa and involves adapting Chinese methods to a very different socio-political environment. It is of symbolic importance and shows that the African leaders are determined to put a real end to the colonial period.

II. PROBLEMS OF PARTICULAR INDUSTRIAL BRANCHES

SOME THOUGHTS ON THE CHOICE AND ADAPTATION
OF TECHNIQUES IN TEXTILE INDUSTRIES

(Background Paper, No. 4)

by

Jacques de Bandt
(Summary)

This paper is based on a number of investigations into the
relative competitivity of textile industries throughout the world.

The analysis of competitivity involves (1) comparisons of
performance (which may vary for the same machinery according to
the way it is used); (2) "quality" and price comparisons of factors; and (3) a combination of (1) and (2), i.e. comparisons of
wage costs and capital costs.

Our reflections have dealt with four successive subjects:
(1) the degree of intensity of the factors in a given production
technique; (2) changes in the relative factor costs; (3) adjustment to the quantitative and qualitative availabilities of factors;
and (4) the conditions of use of second-hand machinery.

Our analysis is exclusively concerned with existing plants
whether old or up-to-date.

Relative intensity of the factors of production

To be competitive one must adjust the proportions of the
required factors to the supplies available, which means choosing
among the available techniques, or evolving a suitable new production technique.

If we exclude the latter alternative and also the possibility
of using second-hand machinery, the effective supply of plant will
be determined to a greater or lesser extent by the demand from producers in the developed countries and the resulting plant will

reflect a growing capital intensity and higher labour productivity.
Judged by purely technical criteria, the machinery will represent
the "best practice techniques".

In cases where the factors of production have a very low substitution elasticity, the production technique can be identified
by their relative intensity. In the case of textiles, low substitution elasticity does not mean that it is not possible to adjust
factor proportions, i.e. to automate the process so as to raise
productivity and so offset high wage rates, but it does mean that
the result can be obtained only at the price of a very substantial
increase in capital costs.

These capital-intensive techniques suit conditions in the
developed countries, but not those in developing countries whose
wage levels are low. They are not the "best practice techniques"
for the latter countries and it would be absurd to try to use them
there.

Thus in the textile industry it is essential to choose production techniques suited to conditions in the developing countries,
if these countries' comparative advantages are not to be lost. The
question is not only a matter of competitivity, but also of collective costs and benefits, volume of employment, aggregate wage bill
and multiplier, external balances and taxation.

Relative factor costs

It is important to minimise the quantities of the most expensive factor, even if more of the cheapest factor has to be used.
In other words, for a given wage level, the higher the cost of
capital, the less advantage there is in using capital-intensive
plant.

An example is given below of the production costs for cotton
fabrics obtained by three different methods, each assuming different wage rates and costs of capital: A - traditional machinery
for use second-hand; B - the most common type of new machinery;
and C - high performance machinery. The hourly wages range from
Frs. 2 to 8 and the average interest rates range from 3 to $7\frac{1}{2}$ per
cent over a 10-year depreciation period.

The minimum production costs (Swiss francs per unit) are as
follows:

Hourly wage	Rate of interest	Method A	B	C
2	3	(169)	(167)	
	7½	179	190	
5	3		219	
	7½		242	
8	3		(271)	255
	7½		294	300

It can be seen from this Table that the optimum technique
is A with minimum wage rates and maximum capital costs, while it
is C with maximum wage rates and a minimum rate of interest.

For a given wage level, the most capital-intensive method
becomes optimum when the rate of interest is lower, while B is the
optimum when wages and rates of interest are both at their lowest
or their highest levels.

Up to now we have assumed that the relative prices constituted a given factor reflecting the relative scarcities of the
factors of production but, if this is true for specific producers,
it does not necessarily hold good at the global level.

In the developing countries relative prices are distorted as
compared with the relative scarcity of factors, so that wages tend
to be higher and rates of interest lower than would correspond to
the real relative scarcity of the factors. The abundance of unskilled labour makes the social cost of labour tend towards zero,
but wages still represent actual expenditure in money. Meanwhile
the cost of capital, which is a scarce factor, is brought down by
development aid and subsidies to industrial investment.

These relative price distortions affect the choice of factor
combinations and encourage higher capital intensity in the manufacturing processes. The systematic subsidisation of capital is
based on the idea that only the most capital-intensive machinery
can be used, which reflects the developed countries' policy of
promoting their own exports.

There is nothing to prevent the subsidies, or part of them,
from being applied to the labour factor so as to reduce wage costs
while not affecting wage incomes. This would make it possible to
increase employment and aggregate wages, to step up competitivity
and to save foreign exchange.

Quantitative and qualitative availabilities of factors

The traditional textile production methods used an abundant
work force, only semi-skilled but relatively specialised, whereas

recent techniques have reduced the numbers of semi-skilled workers, but increased the numbers with higher technical qualifications.

Bearing in mind the low level of labour skill in the developing countries, highly capital-intensive production techniques are introduced so as to reduce labour requirements and the highly skilled manpower needed is recruited from abroad. The alternative is to make the best of one's labour force by trying to make maximum use of the process of apprenticeship and the acquisition of aptitudes for industrial work. The contrast is between a short-term private view and a longer-term social view.

Second-hand machinery

The choice of techniques is limited by the actual supply of plant, which depends mainly on the demand in the developed countries. These countries release considerable amounts of used and written-off machinery, notable for its divisibility and long lease of life.

The machinery to be considered must be relatively recent, if possible under guarantee, and the prestige and other arguments against using it must be disposed of. Its use will considerably widen the possible range of factor combinations. It will involve lower capital expenditure and allow of the least capital intensive combinations, which in some cases will represent the optimum technique. This will be all the more so, the lower the wage rates and the higher the cost of capital, and especially if the relative factor prices have been corrected so as to reflect their real social cost.

Two main conclusions emerge from the above considerations:
1. An economic calculation should be made of the optimum combinations, both by analysing the relative prices and their significance in the light of factor availabilities, and by investigating all the existing technical possibilities, including the use of second-hand machinery.
2. The calculation should not stop at working out a minimum production cost, but should have regard to community interests, including the volume of employment and savings of foreign exchange. Relative prices should therefore be corrected to allow for these factors, so as to make cost prices more compatible with the good of the community.

CHOICE OF TECHNIQUE IN METAL-MACHINING PROCESSES[*]

(Background Paper No. 24)

by

Gérard K. Boon
A Summary Report

Aim

The aim of this study is to investigate the sensitivity of machine optimality on main variables, such as

- capital-labour prices
- size of lots (batches or production runs)
- price of equipment
- price of factory floor space
- number of shifts
- efficiency of labour
- product characteristic
- quality of output.

Scope

Eighty-eight metal-working tasks are formulated (sample established by Rand Corporation, Santa Monica, California, USA).

For 55 tasks two or more alternative machines are listed. For 33 tasks no choice in technique exists. Optimality is calculated for the following alternative parameters:

- Four different sets of capital and labour prices, roughly corresponding with those prevailing in:

  . highly industrialised countries
  . industrialised countries
  . semi-industrialised countries
  . less-industrialised countries.

- Seven different lot size values, ranging from very small to infinite. (The infinite lot size simulates continuous flow production.)

- Two different prices for factory floor space.

---

[*] This report is intended to be a summary presentation of Gérard K. Boon, Employment and Technology, Possibilities and Limitations, to be published.

- Two sets of prices of equipment: one 100 per cent higher than the other.

- Two shift patterns: 8-hour and 16-hour daily operation.

- Two efficiency rates for labour: one USA standard and one 75 per cent of that standard.

Methodology

The criterion for machine optimality is cost minimisation at full utilisation level of machines. Full utilisation is expressed in annual working hours and therefore is influenced by the lot size variable, as well as by the efficiency rate of labour. The model enables to separate the influence of the various variables on machine optimality.

Results of analysis

The study shows that certain metal-machining tasks are sensitive to capital-labour price variation, others more to lot-size variation, while another group is sensitive to both capital-labour and lot-size variation. Finally, certain tasks appear to have fixed coefficients of production. This behavioural pattern can partly be explained by the changes in product- and quality characteristics of the tasks. Three major physical characteristics are distinguished in terms of shape, size and precision.

By way of a generalisation, one can state that the more common the product characteristics are (i.e. non-complex, non-irregular shapes, small to medium size and no extreme requirements on tolerances), the greater is the dependence of technology optimality on lot size. It is possible to create special machines for these tasks, which are so efficient that only the degree of utilisation of these machines determines their optimality. The degree of utilisation is determined, principally, by the scale of production runs and the annual volume of the outputs required. As this might seem a technological explanation, one can also look at the demand or market size for an explanation.

Products which are used in millions are, generally, small and have a high universal applicability. For that reason, their design will evolve to be as functional as possible, both with regard to final use and to their production design. Due to the high and constant demand, it pays to design special purpose equipment for mass production. Such equipment requires, generally, high setting times but very low production times. As the high and constant demand makes large lot size production possible, the total unit production time, defined as the setting time per unit plus the machining and handling time per unit, is relatively so small that unit production costs become competitive regardless of the capital-labour price relation and regardless of the availability of more labour intensive alternatives.

For more complex products, or products generally produced in smaller lot sizes, relative capital-labour prices remain important in the determination of machine optimality. The analysis shows how machine optimality changes, due to the variations in:

   i)   Factor prices
  ii)   The lot sizes and
 iii)   The product characteristics.

If the latter becomes more uncommon due to extreme shapes, sizes of precision requirements, the number of technological alternatives approaches gradually one. Demand for these uncommon products is limited and may be irregular. Mass production is not needed nor possible; lot sizes become small and the choice among alternatives is more and more dictated by the factor price relation.

Also, the relative importance of the other variables for machine optimality is determined keeping lot size and capital-labour prices constant. Increased machine prices, due to import taxes, for example, favours use of more labour-intensive techniques, ceteris paribus. Double shift operation makes use of more capital-intensive techniques, economically preferred, ceteris paribus. Reduced labour efficiency, due to deficient skills, favours more capital-intensive techniques, which rely less on the human element for operation.

Follow-up

The present analysis has been tested on Mexican factories. The outcome has been that for Mexican market prices of production factors, the entrepreneur in the majority of cases chooses the optimal technique as calculated in the study.

Factory visits will be required to examine more closely technology adaptations and capital-intensity of auxiliary operations, such as internal transport.

It could be extremely worthwhile to test the outcome of the analysis also in other countries, such as Brazil and Peru, India and Indonesia, Nigeria and Kenya.

DEVELOPMENT OF APPROPRIATE CHEMICAL
TECHNOLOGY : A PROGRAMME IN MEXICO

(Background Paper No.22)

by

José Giral B.

Chronology

The programme originated some eight years ago, based on the
practical experience acquired in the previous 10 years by the
development and engineering group of the Dupont Company in Mexico
on transfer and adaptation of chemical technology. This programme
was addressed to satisfy two major needs: 1) to better identify
industrial opportunities with a potential for adaptation of technology and 2) to improve the training of the new members of this
development and engineering group.

Three years later (that is, five years ago) the programme
was formally started as an academic research project at the
National University of Mexico, Graduate School of Chemical Engineering, still sponsored by the Dupont Company. Because of the
broadening of the scope beyond the characteristics of a multi-
national corporation the two objectives mentioned above were also
expanded in scope, to cover:

a) consideration of all chemical projects of national
    interest;

b) training in the university as part of the master's
    programme; and

c) implementation of developed appropriate technologies.

In this second stage a morphological or induction analysis
was conducted of the six case stories of successful appropriate
chemical technologies developed by Dupont in Mexico, with a view
to developing a methodology to transform an art into a technique
that may be taught to students and newcomers in this field.

The third stage in the programme is taking place this year.
After a modest success in applying the developed methodology to
three more cases with commercial success, several organisations
became interested in the programme and as a result a working group
was formed by the National University, the Chemical Industry
Association, the Association of Engineering Firms and the Institute

of Chemical Engineers. This group is contributing not only financial resources but, more importantly, expertise on both technological and managerial areas, as well as mechanisms for communication
and implementation of results. Interaction with key government
agencies insures advice and support from the public sectors.

Basic premises

We do not make any distinction between adaptation, innovation
or development of appropriate technology, since we feel these elements are always present and the only thing that affects the semantics is the proportion in which they are present. After all, one
has to keep in mind that the most revolutionary innovations in
chemical technology in the world affected only 10 per cent or less
of that technology, the rest being an adaptation of existing technology. To put it in vulgar terms we feel that the ingredients
needed in this problem are 10 per cent inspiration and 90 per cent
perspiration.

We feel that there is not, by definition, any technological
dependency, but a lack of ability to negotiate because of poor
knowledge of the subject. There is no single chemical technology
that I know where there are not at least three suppliers willing
to provide it.

We consider that in developing appropriate chemical technology
for Mexico the goal should be, on the average, to attain costs at
one-fourth to one-third above the international levels. Our chemical industry currently operates at 70 to 150 per cent above the
international costs. Also, this target cost structure allows for
international competition based on marginal costing, especially
taking into account export incentives, tax subsidies and trade
concessions.

Methodology

In describing the methodology, two general considerations
will be in order:

i)   even though we have classified it in steps, this is an
     iterative process. In other words, one cannot talk of
     product selection without talking of technological or
     process alternatives, which in turn requires knowledge
     of the negotiation terms of each supplier of technology
     and the relationship of risk to cost. One cannot talk of
     transferring a technology without knowing what parts of
     that technology can be adapted either.

ii) One has to keep clearly in mind that the different sec-
    tors of the chemical industry differ widely in the way
    technology is selected, negotiated, transferred and
    adapted. For instance, a converter of plastics can obtain
    his technology by going to the New York plastics show and
    buying an equipment. What the equipment supplier will not
    give him, in terms of technology, he usually obtains from
    the supplier of plastic resin. But in the case of petro-
    chemical industry one cannot obtain so easily know-how
    and one normally ends up buying the process as well as
    the equipment design, and paying large sums both initi-
    ally and as royalties.

Now, our methodology identifies the following seven steps:

1. Selection of plausible products.
2. Selection of base technology.
3. Negotiation of base technology.
4. Transfer of base technology.
5. Adaptation and development of appropriate technology.
6. Feasibility evaluation and
7. Implementation.

We make a distinction between plausible and feasible projects.
We think a project is plausible if it meets the national development objectives and policies. It is feasible if an investor is
willing to put his money into it. To make a highly plausible project feasible, the Government often uses tax and other fiscal
policies or incentives.

For the selection of plausible products we have developed a
checklist of criteria of plausibility. This checklist attempts,
in a very crude form, to provide the Government with a tool to
screen and rank 3,000 to 10,000 chemical products in commercial
use and select 300 to 500 products of potential interest. The
Mexican Department of Industry and Commerce publishes periodically
a list of such products and, for the preparation of the 1973 list,
they will use for the first time our suggested checklist.

The next step is the selection of base technology. From this
step onwards the process is carried out by the enterprise, either
governmental or private. The tools for selection of base technology
are what we call the environmental differences and the technological profiles.

The environmental differences are simply a detailed account of all those advantages and disadvantages that may influence the project. We have developed a checklist that goes from scale of capacity to raw materials, labour, weather, minimum adequate design, legal considerations, etc. The concept is not new by any means, but we feel it is seldom given the high attention it merits, since in our experience this is the richest source of new ideas.

The technological profiles we prepare for 1,100 chemical products take into consideration those criteria that influence the potential of adaptation; for example, whether the process handles gases, liquids or solids; whether it is heterogeneous or homogeneous; whether it has a high or a low energy throughput; etc.

It is important to note that in this step of selection of base technology we consider not only existing commercial technologies but also technologies discarded at the laboratory level or those which have become obsolete many years ago. As a matter of fact, two of our most successful cases stemmed from ideas discarded at the laboratory, and one from an obsolete technology that was up-dated following a different route.

In the third and fourth steps, i.e. negotiation and transfer of technology, we address ourselves to technical aspects only. We are preparing a handbook to assist the negotiating team in identifying the key points that may or may not lend value to a particular technology, and the different packages and level of detail one can buy and transfer. However, even assuming we could do a good job in preparing that handbook, there is nothing I know that can replace the experience on specific technological areas gained through actual negotiation and bargaining.

Another tool we have developed specifically for chemical technology is what we call basic modules language. This tool, of general value throughout the whole methodology, finds its major application in the fifth step: the adaptation and development of an appropriate technology. It consists basically of a language more general than the one used in process flowsheets, more similar perhaps to the language used in the laboratory stage. The major consideration underlying this change of language is that when a chemical engineer defines a process, for example, in terms of a pressure reaction followed by filtration, distillation of a liquid, crystalisation and drying of a solid, he immediately becomes biased as to the type of equipment to use. If, on the other hand, he talks of a chemical transformation followed by a separation of X solid from Y liquid, with adequate details, he can think more easily not only

of filtration but also of many other ways to separate a solid
from a liquid. The emphasis of using this language of basic modules
has produced a noticeable change in the capacity to innovate both
among students and among engineers working in industry and has
provided many valuable ideas to reduce costs and improve efficiency.

At the University we are currently working on a data bank to
feed the basic module language, ranking by different criteria the
alternatives for each basic module.

Because of the lack of time, and since it is perhaps the best
known step, I will not touch on the sixth step, which is the feasibility evaluation of project, except to emphasise the importance
of a risk and sensitivity analysis in supplying meaningful data
for potential investors.

The seventh step of our methodology deals with implementation.
The story of the chemical applied research in Mexico is full of
ideas that look good on paper but have never been implemented. It
is also true, one has to point out, that the story of the Mexican
chemical industry is full of white elephants created by optimistic
technologists and gullible investors. The important point to make
here, and with it I will finish my presentation, is that it is
very important to recognise that appropriate technology developed
or adapted locally is a high risk proposition, balanced by the
potential of a high reward. It is important that the Government
recognises this, that financial institutions accept it, and that
investors have a way to better assess it.

CHOICE AND ADAPTATION OF TECHNOLOGY IN THE FOOD INDUSTRY
(Background Paper No.37)

by

G. Dardenne
(Summary)

The situation in the food industry in the developed countries
can be summed up by two trends: 1) progress in science, technology
and marketing are definitely bringing the industry into the industrial era, and 2) it is developing faster in step with new consumer
requirements (new processes and products).

In the traditional pattern of production in the food industry, one applied generalised techniques to a particular raw material and thereby obtained a product, but today a product is described in terms of marketing requirements and is evolved by research by applying a group of techniques to a series (or combination) of agricultural or non-agricultural raw materials, so leading to an almost infinite range of products.

Factories designed on the basis of a technique are often replaced by factories specialising in a product. The food industry is highly diversified and its market is in reality largely dominated by the multi-national firms.

Many different processes are found inside the same technological family; for example, for deep-freezing one can use plate freezers, tunnels or conveyor-belt equipment. Some processes have been taken over from other industries (e.g. the process for obtaining proteins from soya beans was taken from the textile industry).

The food industry in the developed countries today may be briefly described as follows:

1. As regards working methods, there is a highly organised marketing team which works together with a strong research team and develops more and more elaborate products. The necessary economic, technical and scientific information is obtained from several sources (fundamental research, which is usually government-run; manufacturers of machinery and equipment; firms providing "engineering" or services, etc.). Small firms may play a part, if they can find a niche in the production process.

2. As regards agriculture, some firms have lost touch with agriculture, while others turn to the sources of raw materials for steady supplies of reliable quality (this is the problem of where to locate a firm).

3. As regards machinery, equipment and processes, the producer often makes alterations without informing the manufacturer and the secret of his process is contained more and more in the finished product rather than in the process or machinery he uses.

4. As regards structures, along with powerful firms capable of making large-scale innovations and possessing a world-wide information service, there are supporting firms which

manufacture intermediate products, often specialising in a particular technique or range of products, and usually working as sub-contractors. Medium-scale firms find it difficult to survive owing to their size (the problem of scale). Mass-production has become more and more automated by the use of the latest techniques and a reduced labour force (e.g. in a few years the capacity of a production line for green peas rose from 1-2 tons to 12-20 tons per hour).

The food industries in the developing countries make simple products (usually intermediate products which have to be processed further in the developing countries). These industries have usually been set up with foreign capital and their plant and managerial staff come from abroad. Their labour intensity is low and they are dependent for their technology on the developed countries. As the developing countries have no means of influencing their technology, one cannot really speak of adapting technology (this is true, for example, of the firms which have developed products rich in proteins, even if LDC research establishments have played a part in these projects).

The real problem is how to give LDCs an industry of their own, based on their own agricultural resources, their research facilities and processing capacity, and the markets they hope to win.

a) The raw materials problem. It is necessary to have sufficient quantities of raw materials suitable for processing and also to solve the problems of pricing and stocking them.

b) The human problem. Difficulties arise in changing agricultural manpower into industrial manpower.

c) Technical problems. LDCs depend on other countries for their technology, machinery and equipment. They have the choice between using the techniques current in the developed countries, which are capital-intensive and require little labour, or buying second-hand machinery which is out of date and uncompetitive. There are also problems of infrastructure (water and electricity) to be solved.

d) Market problems. Whether their products are intended for the home market or for export, the developing countries come up against various difficulties: the narrowness of the local market, inability to compete abroad, and the competitive strength and prestige of DC products, which cause them to be preferred to the local products.

Having stated these difficulties, we must now define the rules for an LDC industrial policy:

i) <u>The economic facts</u>. After listing the locally available and imported materials and the locally processed and imported products, an analysis should be made of consumer requirements and after that products should be marketed to replace foreign products and products made by cottage industries. To do this requires a publicity campaign in the countryside and in the towns, paying special attention to the well-to-do classes in the towns.

ii) <u>The technical data</u>. The choice of processes and machinery raises the problem of the need for information and international sources of technical documentation. A board of international sources of technical documentation. A board of economic and technical advisers should be set up in each developing country with access to international sources of information and able to make proposals regarding products, processes, machinery and equipment, etc. In this work it should be assisted by a national committee supported by research establishments.

Stage-by-stage plans should be made and pilot factories could be set up. The "Centro Tropical de Pesquisas en Tecnologia de Alimentos et Campinas" (Brazil) is placing orders for the experimental manufacture of certain products.

Small-scale enterprises, even at handicraft level, could operate alongside larger enterprises set up with government aid, but rather than speak of adapting technology for LDCs where it could only solve minor problems, these countries should take their place in the modern industrial age by solving their real problems, i.e. how to obtain information, choose the right economic options, train and officer the labour force, set up research centres, and design production lines to suit the human factors.

CHOICE AND ADAPTATION OF TECHNOLOGIES IN THE
FOOD INDUSTRY IN DEVELOPING COUNTRIES

(Background Paper No. 16)

by

Jean Torcol
(Summary)

The problems raised by food industries in developing countries should be dealt with under two headings:

a) the establishment of traditional food industries by capitalist groups belonging to industrialised countries. These groups are thoroughly familiar with the techniques which have to be adapted and there is no difficulty in transferring them, so that there is no real technological problem and there seems to us to be no need to intervene in such cases;

b) the establishment of new industries for making products, some of which are also new. Industries of this type use agricultural products as their raw materials, mainly tropical and sub-tropical products (fruits, stimulants, amyloids, etc.) and the most suitable conditions for processing them are not nearly so well known. Considerable research and experimental work must be done before moving on to the industrialisation stage. The techniques which are widely used in industrialised countries for processing fruit juices need to be adapted to suit tropical fruits.

New techniques require to be invented and developed in other fields, in which the industrialised countries have had no particular reason to do research.

A crucial problem for the developing countries is how to store their harvests, from 30 to 40 per cent of which are lost in tropical countries.

Apart from questions of agronomy, a leading part will have to be played by the food technology institutions in industrialising the processing of tropical products.

To sum up, two major steps should be suggested:

i) a list should be made of all the institutions pursuing the same objectives as the ITIPAT in the Ivory Coast;

ii)   periodical meetings of the heads of these institutions
      should be arranged to enable them to exchange experiences,
      explain the work they do and compare results.

EMPLOYMENT AND HOUSING
(Background Paper No.25)

by

Gérard **K**. Boon
(Summary)

When one compares the potential contributions of the different sectors of the economy in this field, one cannot help noticing
the special importance of the construction industry. This sector
offers a wide choice of techniques and is an industry with a
national character which does not usually export and depends but
little on imports. It requires little highly skilled manpower and
so can easily absorb workers from agriculture, for whom it often
acts as a staging post.

Construction, in particular housing construction, is one of
the most labour-intensive industries in the world and most developing countries have to face a shortage of housing, especially for
the lower income brackets. In short, housing construction satisfies
three of the desiderata of the strategy for the Second Development
Decade, namely:

a)   to create jobs,

b)   to make use of labour-intensive techniques, and

c)   to provide improved housing for the workers.

Thanks to the programme of research on this subject carried
out by the OECD Development Centre and the Colegio de Mexico, the
main conclusions arising from experience in this field have been
established.

Stating the problem

One of the purposes of this report was to assess the effects
of a programme of investment in housing construction on the economy
as a whole and in particular on employment.

- 191 -

It was necessary to confine the study to a traditional type of building which was regarded as the most widespread in developing countries, was the most (directly) labour-intensive and was also the most commonly used in Mexico, where the pilot study was being carried out.

Methodology

Having thus defined the scope of the work, several different types of research had to be planned, first at micro-economic level, and then at macro-economic level, after which a way had to be found to establish a relationship between these two levels.

At the micro-economic level, a sample of four types of detached houses was taken, as well as a similar sample for apartment blocks. For each of these eight types of dwelling, average dimensions were assumed and quality standards for the various constituent elements were decided on. After that a detailed list was made of the raw materials used in building 1,000 square metres of each type, showing quantities and 1965 prices.

In order to find out exactly in which stages of building it was possible to vary the techniques, the building process was broken down into steps and for each step a study was made, in co-operation with an architect, of the currently available choice of techniques. These studies showed that there was a wide choice mainly in three operations, namely, preparing the ground and laying the foundations, preparing the cement, and transporting materials up and down (in the case of the apartment blocks). For each of these operations case studies were made to determine the optimum technique and conclusions were drawn regarding the increases or decreases in manpower involved in each different technique.

At the macro-economic level, an input-output model was required to assess the indirect effects of the increased demand for housing on the economic system.

Conclusions

The job-creating effect varies inversely with the cost (or quality) of a dwelling. This applies both to direct employment and to total employment, but the indirect employment varies directly with the quality of the dwelling.

The conclusion is that one can achieve the twofold objective of increasing employment and improving housing conditions for the lower income bracket by a programme of building cheap housing by traditional methods.

The implications of the report for economic policy are the
following:

In the developing countries priority should be given to encouraging the building of low-cost housing or medium-quality housing, paying special attention to using cheap locally-produced
materials. This will lead, not only to increased total employment,
but also to reduced imports of intermediate products and a lower
volume of investment. Private contractors should be encouraged to
use labour-intensive techniques.

In view of the considerable effects of this policy on total
consumption, attention must be paid to the elasticity of the supply of staple consumer goods so as to avoid inflationary pressure.

Adaptation of technologies may, in general, be of three types,
involving: production techniques, the product itself, and the raw
materials, with various feed-back effects.

In Mexico the major changes in techniques are the results of
the climate, which is either temperate or sub-tropical and calls
for a lighter type of construction. The water mains are of a lower
quality and do not need to be insulated. The techniques as a whole
show the influence of the old Spanish tradition (bricks, but little
wood, which is rather expensive).

This survey was intended to cover only Mexico, and it might
usefully be extended to other countries. Interesting comparisons
might be made, which might reveal new ways of adapting local techniques involving various substitution processes.

CONDITIONS FOR INDUSTRIALISING HOUSING CONSTRUCTION
IN FRENCH-SPEAKING AFRICA

(Background Paper No. 17)

by

Michel Gérard
(Summary)

A number of setbacks are found in housing construction in
developing countries today, and especially in French-speaking
Africa, due to the brutal introduction of imported highly industrialised techniques.

A major anomaly is that there is a modern sector, which only a minute section of the population can afford because of its price, rubbing shoulders with a more easily accessible traditional sector, but without any connection between the two or co-operation between contractors in them. Yet the income curves for the countries in question clearly show that, the lower the level of development, the less effective will efforts be to improve productivity in the modern sector, and that even a large reduction in costs will not put this sector within the reach of more than a few additional households. By contrast, only a slight reduction in costs in the traditional sector will bring in a considerable number of new customers.

a) <u>Improving the productivity of the traditional building industry at the purely technical level</u>. This often appears to be a simple matter, but one must not overlook other aspects (the problem of the small contractor's cash resources, etc.). At all events it seems necessary to try to give training and further training to building workers in their traditional techniques, since the know-how in the latter, which are of peasant origin, is lost by the generations of town-dwellers and one ends up with shanty town techniques.

b) <u>Production of sub-assemblies for buildings</u>. For the interior work in buildings builders at the pre-industrial stage should be given guidance based on market studies and encouraged (other than by the traditional financial constraints) to use local materials rather than imported materials (e.g. galvanised steel sheets, locks, and the like). With regard to the main fabric and the actual building materials, one comes up against psychological obstacles, e.g. the preference for cement as compared to brick (which could have a great future in Africa) and to wood which is regarded as a low class material. An effort should be made to put up prestige buildings of brick and, especially, of wood.

c) <u>The supply of more or less fully equipped building sites</u> (infrastructure), which are at least as important as the houses themselves. Here again one comes up against psychological obstacles; sometimes people can imagine these sites as prepared to take only modern-style dwellings, but at other times they think that the infrastructure work, which can be expensive, should be done free of charge for the masses.

A land development policy should also be worked out to prevent the speculation which might be encouraged by the economic climate created by a housing shortage. One might cite here the IBRDs experiments in Morocco and Senegal.

In this connection the transfer and adaptation of technology raises two major problems, namely, the risk that information which is passed on without being adapted to suit the economy of the recipient will become an instrument of "mental colonisation"; and the same risk when using "engineering" services which are not thoroughly specialised in the area concerned, e.g. Africa. The solution would be to set up local "engineering" services staffed by nationals of the country who could correspond with "engineering" offices, which had some specialised knowledge, in the industrialised countries. In this connection the industrialised countries themselves should make an effort to adapt their techniques for use in other environments.

In conclusion it is proposed:

i)   that both sides should get to know each other better;

ii) that techni-economic centres should be set up and multiplied;

iii) that a search should be made for entrepreneurs in the developed countries who are interested in adapting technology;

iv) that a large-scale propaganda campaign should be launched in the industrialised countries to bring these problems home to them.

III. GENERAL TOPICS

LARGE MULTI-NATIONAL FIRMS AND TRANSFER OF TECHNOLOGY
(Background Paper No. 33)

·by

P. Judet and C. Palloix

(Summary)

It is generally agreed by economists and authorities in international organisations that the large multi-national firms, which usually have extensive research facilities and the ability to innovate, are an effective medium for transferring technology from the developed countries (DCs) to the developing countries (LDCs).

To see whether this idea is sound, one should look into the internationalisation process which gives rise to the new industrialisation policy and consists in internationalising the three activities which make up an industry, i.e.:

a) the production process
b) the commercial product
c) the distribution process.

This internationalisation process exhibits three tendencies:

1) There is a tendency for a technological process to be imposed by the leading multi-national firms on the industry concerned in all countries and to become the dominant process. This has happened, for example, in steel-making, where plants situated on the water's edge are seen to rule supreme; in mechanical and electrical engineering, which are dominated by General Electric, Westinghouse and Brown-Boveri; in petro-chemicals, etc.

2) The transition from a "products" strategy to one of packages of goods and services. While the product has no direct connection with the market, the package is a combination of goods and services which fits a market. For

example, the large firms are no longer producing just pipes or furnaces, but complete pipework systems and heat treatment installations. These packages need an international stage and we find the multi-national firms making a general movement downstream towards the market. The petro-chemical firms produce first petro-chemicals and then synthetic fibres, and they even bid fair to control the output of the final product (apparel). The end result of this trend is the supply of turn-key plants.

3) The third tendency is for the international trading companies to control the international networks for distributing goods. In Japan, for example, the nine leading trading companies handled 46.7 per cent of Japan's exports and 59.7 per cent of its imports in 1970.

Industries are restructured so as to capture the market and control the international distribution networks rather than to satisfy purely technical criteria (economic considerations outweigh technical considerations).

The "engineering" firms play a part in this process by ensuring the supremacy of the major firms' technical processes and by assembling products into marketable packages (power stations, turn-key plants, etc.)

Having said this, we must enquire whether the multi-national firms are an important medium for transferring technology.

It should first be realised that many LDC industrial plants were put up by the large multi-national firms, so that transfers of technology have actually taken place.

These transfers were made, however, without adapting the techniques to their new environment because multi-national firms have a different viewpoint from local firms and prefer to use a more up-to-date technology which they know and thoroughly understand rather than embark on a process of adapting it to an unknown or little known environment. In any case, the main object of the multi-national firm is never to transfer and adapt technology, but instead to develop the international network for distributing the goods it controls by extending that network to cover the developing countries.

This failure to adapt technology creates or strengthens a tendency in developing countries to make their economies outward-looking. Indeed, it is difficult not to see the strategy of the multi-national firms in the policy now being advocated for these countries to set up "export-oriented" industries.

The multi-national firms cause traditional inter-industry
relations to be broken off, after which they pick up the threads
and establish their own relations, for their own benefit and under
their own control (e.g. the transfer of certain polluting processes
upstream to Spain, Greece or Yugoslavia). Local sub-contracting,
which is the basis of the industrial fabric, gives way to international sub-contracting. Experience in the Italian Mezzogiorno
shows that there are hardly any links between the newly established
production units, but instead there are links between each unit
(making "products") and its parent firm in Northern Italy or abroad.

Thus one must distinguish between appearance and reality in
the process of transferring technology via the large firms. There
is the appearance of a transfer of technology, but in reality the
economies of the developing countries are made outward-looking and
they become linked up with the strategies of the multi-national
firms, which then capture and control them.

The main feature of this process is the primacy of economic
interests over technological interests. The transfers of technology
made by the large multi-national firms <u>include no transfer of ability to innovate</u>. Innovation always depends on being in the right
economic environment and here it is always the large firms at
international level which provide the environment.

In conclusion one may say that the multi-national enterprises
aggravate the outward-looking tendencies of the economies of the
developing countries by tying them in with their overall strategy.
The operations of such enterprises alone cannot bring about industrialisation in these countries. It must be based on foundations
built at home, on an inward-looking economy and on quite a different strategy.

SETTING UP "ENGINEERING" FIRMS IN THE INDUSTRIALISING
COUNTRIES AS AGENTS FOR TRANSFERRING KNOW-HOW
(Background Paper No. 34)

by

J. Perrin
(Summary)

In recent years a separation has had to be made between the
work of designing and constructing a plant "engineering" and its

production operations, this work being handled separately by design departments and groups of engineering consultants and, more recently, by specialised or diversified "engineering" firms.

"Engineering" has close relations with other industrial activity (R and D, production, the manufacture of plant, and financial institutions) of which it has need to carry out the different stages of a project, viz. the preliminary studies, the pre-project studies, the detailed project studies, the implementation plans, purchase and inspection, assembly and installation, and starting up the project.

These relations are not only one-way. For example, "engineering" needs to know the results of the R and D, which provide it with data on processes, but it in turn is able to identify the problems requiring research and to translate the results into economic terms. "Engineering" is the medium both for accumulating and for disseminating industrial experience and as such it is able to advise plant manufacturers and contractors, but it will always be more closely connected with certain particular manufacturers. Thus the nationality of an "engineering" service is of decisive importance, since foreign services do not know the plant manufacturers in the developing country.

Information plays an important part in "engineering" which we define as the whole body of methods and organisational structures with which one can master the scientific, technical and economic information required for converting capital into a coherent set of productive forces.

The second industrial revolution is distinguished by the use of information, just as the first revolution was based on the law of the conservation of energy, and the independent status of "engineering" is explained by a new division of labour due to the new productive force furnished by scientific and technical information. In some industries (chemicals, petro-chemicals and cement) the design and construction (and also the maintenance) are more important than the production stage proper.

It is in this context that one must approach the problem of transferring or rather mastering technology. In the developing countries the investing is generally done by foreign "engineering" firms on a turn-key basis, and the local "engineering" firms which exist in some of these countries have great difficulty in obtaining the design information they require. The developing countries must therefore master this "engineering" work and consequently solve the information problem in order to master the technology.

According to the definition of Russo and Urbes, information is a flow of knowledge from the informant to the recipient via a written, audible or visible medium, but it must be stressed that knowledge can be acquired without information (discovery, intuition, and knowledge acquired by practical experience) and that by processing information one can obtain new information which is more detailed and operational. Know-how can only be acquired by experience and contact with the actual conditions being studied.

The "engineering" firms collect and process various information:

i)   scientific and technical information concerning the process, which includes some know-how;

ii) manufacturing information (monitoring and control equipment, automated systems with or without computers, etc.);

iii) information on the geographical environment (climate, transport facilities, terrain, etc.);

iv) information on the economic environment (manpower, housing, terms and conditions of finance and payments, taxation, etc.);

v)   design information (including information on building and construction techniques);

vi) information on plant and plant manufacturers (choice of plant, inspection, etc.).

In addition to these different kinds of know-how (concerning processes, plant and design) there is another kind directly connected with the teamwork involved in an "engineering" firm which employs several specialists. For example, it is generally agreed that a firm cannot add more than 10 per cent of new recruits to its staff per year without the danger of upsetting the smooth progress of its operations.

Developing countries which wish to set up rapidly their own "engineering" services will have to acquire their expertise and know-how in the developed countries. It is possible for them to obtain the expertise by means of a dynamic education and training policy and by buying licences, but how to acquire know-how is a more complicated matter and can only be done by recruiting one or more persons or co-operating with a foreign firm.

Let us now examine how different kinds of know-how are acquired, with reference to some studies we have made on the development of "engineering" in India and Algeria.

Process know-how

Not only "engineering", but also, and even more, the R and D facilities in a country stand to gain from acquiring this kind of know-how. In India, the Central Engineering and Design Bureau (CEDB) belonging to the public sector Hindustan Steel Ltd. has benefited from studies made by the National Metallurgical Laboratory. As regards fertiliser, the two Indian producers in the public sector each have an "engineering" department, the Planning and Development Division (P and D) for the Fertiliser Corporation of India, and the Engineering and Design Organisation (FEDO) for the Fertiliser and Chemicals of Travencore. P and D employs 1,400 persons and looks after R and D and the planning and construction of fertiliser plants, acting also (as does the FEDO) as an engineering consultant.

What these two Indian organisations lack, however, is the ability to adapt the foreign processes acquired by buying licences to practical requirements. This failing is not peculiar to developing countries and is also found in France, but it should be pointed out that it is a weakness of "engineering" which casts doubt on the whole R and D policy.

Plant know-how

It is the job of the plant manufacturers to acquire this kind of know-how and the "engineering" of the country concerned should help them by placing orders with them, making technical suggestions to them, etc. Although "engineering" can exist without the support of a plant manufacturing sector, the latter will help it to develop more quickly and easily than when all the plant is imported. The two-way flow of communications which will take place in the former case between "engineering" and manufacturers will not be possible in the latter case.

Know-how in technical studies and "engineering" organisations

These two kinds of know-how are mainly required by "engineering" and concern especially the detailed studies stage of projects, when the developing countries encounter more difficulties than in the preceding stages covering the preliminary studies and pre-project studies.

Various arrangements have been tried by the developing countries, and in particular by Algeria, for acquiring these two kinds of know-how.

The SNS iron and steel complex at El Hadjar set up a new project service with an implementation planning office working as sub-contractor to foreign "engineering" services. The SNS tried out different working arrangements with foreign "engineering" firms, but without much success, and ended up by recruiting some specialised engineers directly to train its own "engineering" staff, giving the latter full responsibility for some less complex sub-assemblies tube-coating shops, general and administration services, etc.). In India the CEDB and the P & D followed a similar course in developing their "engineering" services.

From these examples certain conclusions may be drawn:

i)   it is not in the nature of things for a foreign "engineering" firm to help its competitors in developing countries;

ii) there is a clash between good planning and meeting date-lines on the one hand and training requirements on the other.

Only by giving direct responsibility for projects to a national system of "engineering" services can one reconcile an "engineering" firm's responsibilities with training requirements. One can either incorporate in the system a team of foreigners supplied by an "engineering" firm in a developed country, or engage foreign specialists on an ad hoc basis depending on the projects to be carried out, even if this arrangement cannot solve all the difficulties. In any case, however, such arrangements assume that the developing country possesses a fairly coherent national structure and sufficient qualified staff.

The developing countries, faced as they are with the problems of transferring expertise and know-how, would certainly find it useful to have a more detailed analysis of these problems, which we have done no more than mention.

THE TRANSFER OF TECHNOLOGY AND CONDITIONS FOR INDUSTRIALISATION IN THE THIRD WORLD

(Background Paper No. 26)

by

Moises Ikonicoff
(Summary)

Since the fifties the developing countries have seen their productivity increased and their consumption patterns brought up to date for the benefit of a minority of the population and without helping to promote technical progress. The main features of this period were the dependence of these countries on the developed countries and their inability to spread the new patterns of consumption to the whole population.

It cannot be denied, however, that the developing countries have done much to industrialise, since the annual rate of growth of their manufacturing industry rose from 3.8 per cent in 1938/50 to 6.9 per cent in 1950/52 and then to 7.5 per cent in 1957/65. Nevertheless, the typical distortions found in under-development have not disappeared, and it is now believed that the process of transferring technology gives rise to new distortions and arrests growth.

Technology is not neutral and technology for export has been planned by and for the developed countries to suit the factors of production and natural resources they possess. This is why the plant exported to the developing countries is capital-intensive and not labour-intensive and why, for example, the developed countries transfer processes for the iron and steel industry based on the use of coal as a reducer and not natural gas, which would suit the developing countries better.

Technology costs (direct and indirect) are high and in some cases mean that enterprises in developing countries are taken over by multi-national firms.

It is in order to mitigate these unfavourable effects of transferring technology that attention has been given to organising new ways of transferring it at international level and free from control by private firms.

Many proposals have been made for organising the exchange and spread of technical information so as to make it available to the countries able to use it, but without subjecting them to the

constraints imposed by private contracts for transferring technology. For example, it has been proposed that a technical data bank
should be set up under the patronage of the international organisations.

The transfer of technology is not an entirely exogenous phenomenon imposed from outside, but obeys special principles underlying the working of economic mechanisms.

As industrialisation benefits only a minority of the population of the developing countries, it is the growth in this minority's demand which leads to imports of technology and this in turn
aggravates the distortions and inequalities in the economy, so that
it is a mistake to discuss the transfer of technology in terms of
national boundaries.

The same phenomenon occurs when one proceeds to the import-
substitution stage and even after this stage. Production remains
conditioned by the demand of a minority and, in the final stage,
the powers of decision pass more and more to the large multi-
national firms and their subsidiaries in the developing countries.

To sum up, the traditional approaches should be replaced by
a new strategy based on increased efficiency in using resources
and on preventing the introduction of new products.

In this case, (1) the cumulative process will tend to be
speeded up, and (2) there will be an increasing tendency for consumption patterns to become standardised.

INDUSTRIAL DEVELOPMENT IN RELATION TO INDUSTRIAL SATISFACTION
(Background Paper No. 18)

by

Daniel Carrière
(Summary)

Two premises emerge from our observations concerning industry
and enterprises:

Premise 1 : the industrial firm in the development satisfaction or degradation stage and the opportunities for concluding
agreements among firms;

Premise 2 : migrant workers and the capacity for technological adaptation.

The first premise deals with the factors and the second premise with the actors in adapting technology.

Premise 1

The industrial firm passes through three successive stages, namely development, satisfaction and industrial degradation, corresponding to the stages when it is set up, when it makes good and wins independence, and lastly when it declines because it can no longer overcome some economic, technological and social constraints.

These three stages are found in all economic systems, which is why the problem of choosing and adapting technology must be studied, not only with reference to the developing countries, but also with reference to the enterprises in the developed countries which are living in the satisfaction stage, but are in constant danger of degradation.

Premise 2

Migrant workers have always acted as channels of communication and technical training, but the place given them in the host countries relegates them to the position of "passive" agents for adapting technology, the service organisations (consultants, "engineering" firms, etc.) being the only "active" agents in the adaptation process, although they do not always take much interest in it.

The main factors in choosing and adapting technology are the following:

a) complementarities in production;
b) the language used in communicating technology information; and
c) the recognition and self-assertation of different technological environments.

a) Because enterprises which have reached maturity have gaps and weaknesses, it is possible to redistribute activities between them and enterprises at the development stage, thus transferring know-how and expertise and also sharing the risks. The weak points include the widely diversified range of products, manpower shortages in certain industries, the wide variety of shapes and sizes of products, the limits to the use of machinery, etc.

b) Technical language should be changed and adapted, information should be broken down into its various component parts, and communication between sectors and countries should be encouraged by fighting against the dispersal and waste of information.

c) The different technological environments must be able to assert themselves and they must be given the right to innovate and also to make mistakes and suffer setbacks, without which there can be no progress. Finally, bridges must be built between the different technological environments so that the confrontations required for a creative approach may take place.

The most important actors in choosing and adapting technology are the enterprises and the migrant workers, and they must be given the means to play an "active" part instead of the "passive" part now allotted to them.

In conclusion, practical proposals for dealing with these various points should be discussed, as follows:

Complementarities

Can the existing centres of technology lead to setting up mutual associations for industrial development? Are agreements possible which are not based on some dependent relationship, either in a standard form for each industry or otherwise? Which enterprises would be affected by such agreements (the small and medium-sized firms, the multi-national firms, etc.)? What would be the criteria for choosing the technologies to be transferred under these agreements?

Languages for communicating technological information

Might not information be transmitted to enterprises irrespective of their stage of development? Might no existing technical data banks be interlinked through the agency of UNIDO or an International Mutual Association for Industrial Development? Should not centralised question-and-answer facilities be set up which would draw on a variety of resources (e.g. the reviews Usine Nouvelle, Chemical Abstracts, etc.)?

Enterprises

How can enterprises be made to understand the value of negotiating reciprocal agreements? How should one determine the dimensions and minimum levels warranting the negotiation of such agreements? Can one make a study of existing agreements of this kind and encourage other enterprises to follow their example?

Migrant workers

How can the skills of migrant workers be used for adapting technology? Should not Creativity Institutes be set up by and for these workers and a healthy confrontation be arranged between them and resident workers?

THE PROBLEM OF TRANSFERRING TECHNOLOGY FROM
BRANCH TO BRANCH AND THE MULTIPLIER

(Background Paper No. 14)

by

Jean Parent
(Summary)

The advanced technologies have been developed in a few industrial countries and they form a coherent pattern and complete each other. Thus to solve certain problems in one industry one must assume and ensure that the problems in other industries are solved also.

Each branch, in fact, produces linkage effects which spread to other apparently quite unconnected industries. They may be quantitative (resembling multiplicator effects) and they will then depend on several factors including the importance of the originating industry in total industrial production, the number of its direct connections with the other industries and the number of industries affected which are really operating in the country. If the supporting industries are missing, attempts to establish leading industries will fail.

However, the linkage effects may also be technological, due to the ability of an industry to "oblige" other industries to make technical alterations. They mainly follow on the quantitative effects and also depend on the importance of the originating industry and the number of its direct connections. The more use a buying industry makes of a complex technology, the more exacting will be its demands (e.g. the aerospace industry). An industry A (the supplier) will be the more dependent technologically on an industry B, the more of its output it sells to that industry.

In the developing countries the major industries often have to adapt their technology to the requirements of buying industries in the developed countries (e.g. the extraction of minerals).

However, there are other channels for transmitting incentives:

a) from upstream downstream: supplies of new types of raw materials and plant give rise to changes in the buying industries;

b) linkage effects may also be produced horizontally, when their constituent forces will influence one another;

c) industries which do little business with one another may tend to copy or infect each other.

One will thus find leading industries and "cross-roads" industries, the former being centres of technical progress which they pass on to the others, and the latter acting as transfer agents for satisfying requirements felt in a number of different quarters. The leading industries are often "cross-roads" industries also, and vice-versa. These industries are distinguished by two main features:

i) a complex technology which usually involves many inter-connections and exacting requirements (leading industries, such as aeronautics or nuclear engineering);

ii) the quantitative importance of interconnections which require a major development of complementary industries ("cross-roads" industries, e.g. the building industry and motor vehicles).

In the developing countries there are few transfers of technology from one industry to another and the problems of industrial organisation must be restated in terms of complementary technological groups. The main question requiring an answer is the following: What industries should be set up in the near future to improve the capacity of a given industry to develop?

AN EXPERIMENT IN INTERNATIONAL TRANSFER OF TECHNOLOGY: PILOT PROJECT FOR LATIN AMERICA

(Background Paper No. 8)[*]

by

Organisation of American States (OAS)
(Abstract)

A technical development policy requires an adequate combination of:

- development of an internal balanced system of research, education, information and technical extension services (supply of domestic technology);

- development of a capability for technical innovation (demand for technology);

- an adequate process of importation of technologies through proper selection, adaptation, application and improvement of imported technologies; as well as an export promotion of technologies (technology trade).

The domestic scientific and technical infrastructure should be integrated into the technology and transfer process actively participating in it.

The OAS conducted an analysis of the technological market from the view-point of the exporters of technology and from the view-point of the Latin American importers, which revealed the following major elements:

a) The linkage between the government, the industry, the scientific and technological system and the financing sector is missing almost completely in Latin America.

b) There is scarce demand for technical change and this demand, when arising, is satisfied by imports of technology.

c) The present technological dependence will further increase unless structural measures are taken to reinforce the scientific and technical system and to modify the present process of transfer of technology;

---

[*] This abstract is based on the modified version written by Mr. Maximo Halty-Carrère, November 1972.

d) Technology is a commodity with special characteristics and its buyers face various problems (overpricing, restrictive conditions, inadaptability to local conditions).

e) There is a tendency to sell "packaged technology" with the extreme case of "turn-key plants"

f) the national scientific and technological system participates only marginally in the process of transfer of technology.

g) Deficiency or absence of systems of information on existing alternative technologies, lack of criteria for the selection of them, and inability to adapt foreign technologies, to generate local ones and to negotiate in the international technological market.

These aspects constituted the basis of the OAS Pilot Project for Transfer of Technology, which aims at improving the process of transfer of technology to and within Latin America. The project has been formulated for a two-year experiment concentrating on the following functions : information on technological alternatives, evaluation and selection of existing technologies and assistance to the negotiation for the purchase of technology.

An inter-connected network at the regional and the national level will conduct the project; this network includes the National Focal Points (NFP) and the Regional Focal Point (RFP).

The NFPs will organise the participation of each country in the Project, through the identification of the participating enterprises, the establishment of a communication link between these enterprises and the RFP and provide technological information and assistance to these enterprises.

Moreover, the project attempts to evolve a new mechanism of co-ordination between the government and the technological, financial and productive systems. The co-ordinating staff of the project should include representatives from all these sectors.

The RFP will organise and guide the project to achieve its objectives, will co-ordinate the exchange of information and experiences between the participating countries and will supply them with technological information.

The Pilot Project will cover three main industrial sectors: food technology, chemical industry and basic metal industries, but some 20 per cent of the budget will be reserved for "free projects" outside these sectors.

The "technical problems" which involve technology requirements will be examined by means of technological profiles, summaries and prospectus.

The execution of the project will be divided into two stages: during the first stage the existing technological requirements will be processed and in the second stage the technological requirements corresponding to the detected implicit demand will be dealt with.

Fourteen Latin American countries will participate in the project (Argentina, Brazil, Bolivia, Colombia, Chile, Ecuador, Peru, Uruguay, Venezuela, Costa Rica, El Salvador, Guatemala, Honduras and Nicaragua). Not only certain UN agencies and other inter-governmental organisations, but several developed countries (USA, Canada, United Kingdom, Italy, Japan, etc.), are expected to support the project technically and financially.

IV. INDUSTRIAL INFORMATION

CHOICE AND ADAPTATION OF TECHNOLOGY IN DEVELOPING COUNTRIES
(Background Paper No. 9)

by

Mohamed Daya
(Summary)

If the developing countries are to be able to choose and adapt technology, they must have available a range of choices.

In point of fact, the developing countries' first problem has been to find employment for large reserves of manpower by investing in industries which were sometimes of doubtful profitability and often based on a wrong choice of technology. In addition, the "engineering" firms commissioned to make the technico-economic studies were often connected with plant manufacturers and slanted their reports towards the choice of certain processes and types of plant.

One is always faced by the alternative of choosing either a less advanced technology to absorb the available manpower, which is often unskilled and even illiterate, or a more advanced technology with which goods can be produced for export.

Some examples may be mentioned of technical mishaps caused by the unsuitability of the technology chosen: an esparto pulp factory for which the plans and main items of plant had to be changed; a fruit juice enterprise which never reached the stage of effective production; a sulphuric acid plant based on a local raw material involving excessive costs of production; and a mechanical engineering plant which took ten years of adjustment to reach normal output. All these enterprises were financed with tied aid.

The following conclusions may be drawn from these setbacks:

a) the developing countries are not yet properly equipped to make a sound choice of technologies;

b) the "engineering" firms keep their secrets jealously and are not always prepared to pass them on to others;

c) tied aid is not the ideal background for choosing the right technology.

The answer to the question whether to choose a less advanced but labour-intensive technology or a more advanced but capital-intensive technology is that in practice one must steer a judicious course between the two.

It is not a solution to use second-hand machinery, because even if it calls for less investment it leads to an increase in production costs and widens still more the technological gap between the developed and the developing countries.

The position in the Maghreb countries is that they are capable of making use of all the technical expertise in the world, but are handicapped by the prevailing arrangements for transferring technology and by the restrictions imposed by the owners of processes (restricted rights to export, to improve a process, etc.). An example of the evils in these arrangements is a fertiliser plant which spent $2 million on buying a process which in the end it did not use.

In addition to the handicaps of inadequate transfers of technology already mentioned (tied aid and inaccessibility of sources of information) one might mention the socio-economic structure handed down by history.

In conclusion, steps should be taken at three levels to remedy the situation:

a) national technology cells should be created which would contain documentation and economic, scientific and technical information services and could exploit and disseminate technological information;

b) regional technology cells should be created with the task of exploiting and transferring technologies of value to a given area;

c) a technology service should be established at the international level which could help the developing countries to set up national technology cells and train skilled personnel.

THE ROLE OF INFORMATION IN THE TRANSFER OF
TECHNOLOGY - AN EXPERIMENT IN MEXICO

(Background Paper No. 32)

by

The Technical Information Service of the
National Science and Technology Council of Mexico (CONACYT)

(Abstract)

The National Science and Technology Council of Mexico
(Consejo Nacional de Ciencia y de Tecnologia - CONACYT) set up a
national scientific and technical information and documentation
network in Mexico which includes 30 institutions working together
in order to co-ordinate the library system, to design a telex network, to update the union catalogue of serials, training personnel,
etc.

One of the main components of the CONACYT programme is the
industrial Information System intended to identify the demand for
information and to supply the available information from Mexico
and abroad to the industrial sector. CONACYT acts as a central
clearing house among the different specialised information centres
in the fields of electricity, chemistry, metallurgy, etc.

The Industrial Information System includes three main services
working in different directions:

   i)   the Technical Information Service;
  ii)   the Technical Inquiry Service; and
 iii)   the Technical News Service.

The Technical Information Service is specially concerned with
small and medium sized industrial firms and includes:

a)   a technical inquiry service which is promoted by visits
    to these firms and supplies them with adequate information
    to solve their problems;

b)   a monthly information dissemination service, which pub-
    lishes a monthly bulletin prepared by 8 engineers contain-
    ing abstracts of selected technical articles.

The Technical Inquiry Service started in January 1972 and the
enquiries received are increasing at a very fast rate. This service
uses such instruments as descriptor lists, the Engineering Index,

the Chemical Abstracts, etc., and eventually contacts international organisations, such as UNIDO, if the information required is not available in Mexico.

The Technical News Service is provided to 300 firms in the chemical, metal mechanic, electrical, food and glass industries. Each company receives a monthly bulletin containing 20 articles related to its industry and two common bulletins on administration and pollution. All the articles selected are computerised.

CONACYT intends to develop its activities, namely by creating a documentation service for industry, a close liaison service between industry and research by collecting information on specialists, consultants and technical advisors, etc.

VOLUNTEERS IN TECHNICAL ASSISTANCE (VITA)
(Background Paper No. 23)

by

Thomas Fox
(Abstract)

Volunteers in Technical Assistance (VITA) is a private non-profit organisation established in 1960 to respond to requests for technical assistance in economic and social development projects.

At first, VITA worked through various missionary and international service groups with field representatives in the developing world. A full time staff was created in 1965 to administer all incoming requests. The staff co-ordinator is responsible for providing overseas requestors, public and private, with appropriate technical assistance through the use of individual volunteer resources and a network of public and private agencies. Each co-ordinator is specialised in a specific geographic area (Asia, Africa, Latin America).

VITA has worked closely with OECD-DES (146 requests have been answered in 1972) and with the UNIDO-I.I.S. (256 UNIDO cases have been serviced by VITA the same year).

The heart of VITA operation is its membership, which now comprises over 6,000 scientists, engineers, businessmen, agriculturalists and educators who volunteer their spare time to provide technical assistance by mail to people in developing countries. They represent some 1,800 corporations, universities and other organisations and their skills in commerce, industry, health, education, engineering, etc. have been applied to more than 25,000 requests (2,500 a year). About 50 per cent of the requests deal with industrial and technological problems.

VITA has a publication programme, which includes the <u>Village Technology Handbook</u> and a number of manuals and technical guides in several languages.

ANNEXES

I. ORDER OF DISCUSSIONS

Note: numbers in brackets after the names of speakers refer to Background Paper.

Tuesday 7th November: a.m.

1. Opening session: Agenda procedures, election of **Rapporteurs** and other administrative matters.

2. Agenda Item A: (Appropriate technology and development strategy).

   Topics for introductory speakers:

   i) Terminological review and duality - F. Stewart (11)

   ii) Duality and development stages - G. Ranis (introduced and commented by Mr. Usui) (5)

   iii) Appropriate technology for the non-modern sector - B. Behari and K. L. Nanjappa (19, 20 and 38)

   iv) Multi-national firms and the LDC modern sector - P. Judet (33)

GENERAL DISCUSSION

Tuesday 7th November: p.m.

3. Agenda Item B: (Policy appraisals at the national level)

   Topics for introductory speakers:

   i) Main features of the science policy studies in OECD countries - F. Chesnais.

   ii) Methodologies of the UNESCO science policy studies - M. Chapdelaine.

   iii) A general model of technology transfer mechanism envisaged in the OAS pilot project - P. Gonod (8)

iv) Technology and factor prices - J. de Bandt (4)

v) Indicators of technological development -
M. Chapdelaine.

vi) Technology assessment methodology for LDCs -
G. F. Schweitzer (35)

vii) Micro-analysis on the choice of production techniques -
G. Boon (24)

DISCUSSION

Wednesday 8th November: a.m.

4. Agenda Item C: (Policy studies related to specific branches
of industry)

Topics for introductory speakers:

i) Food industries - J. Torcol (16), G. Dardenne (37)

ii) Chemical industries - J. Giral (22)

iii) Engineering - J. Perrin (34)

iv) Housing - M. Gerard (17), G. Boon (25)

DISCUSSION

Wednesday 8th November: p.m.

Agenda Item D: (Actors and factors responsible for successes
and failures)

Topics for introductory speakers

i) Industrial and technological information services.
The following speakers outlined the organisation with
which they are concerned:

M. Daya (9)
R. Kraetsch
B. Behari (1)
A. Latham-Koenig (15)
K. Nanjappa (38)
J. Fernandez (32)
T. Fox (23)
J. Stepanek
M. Gerard (17)

<u>Thursday 9th November</u>: a.m.

     <u>Further general discussion of information services</u>

       ii) Reviews of on-going and planned projects

            a) NAS appropriate technology studies - S. Teitel.

            b) MIT programme for technology adaptation - J. Ruina.

            c) "Soft" technology - P. Harper.

            d) OAS pilot project for technology transfer -
                P. Gonod (8)

            e) "International Institute for Industrialisation" -
                J. Stepanek.

<u>Thursday 9th November</u>: p.m.

  Rapporteurs' summing up.

CONCLUDING DISCUSSION

Edmundo de ALBA,
Director, Studies and Support Services,
Consejo Nacional de Ciencia y Tecnologia,
Insurgentes Sur 1677,
Mexico 20 D.F.
Mexico

José ALMEIDA,
I.P.E.A.,
Rua Melvin Jones, 5,
Rio de Janeiro, GB.,
Brazil

Jacques de BANDT,
Directeur,
Institut de Recherche en Economie de la Production,
(U.E.R. de Sciences Economiques)
2, rue de Rouen,
92 Nanterre
France

Bepin BEHARI,
Joint-Director, Appropriate Technology Cell,
Ministry of Industrial Development,
Government of India,
268 Udyog Bhavan,
New Delhi,
India

Gerard K. BOON,
Consultant,
El Colegio de Mexico,
Guanajuato 125,
Mexico 7, D.F.,
Mexico

W. BREDO,
Director,
International Development Center,
Stanford Research Institute,
Menlo Park,
California 940025,
USA

Daniel **CARRIERE**,
Consultant OECD/UNIDO,
2, Allée des Dahlias,
93 Drancy,
France

Marc CHAPDELAINE,
Department of Science Policy and Promotion of Basic Sciences,
UNESCO,
Place de Fontenoy, 7ème,
France

Roland COLIN,
Directeur Générale,
I.R.F.E.D.,
49, rue de la Glacière,
Paris 13ème,
France

Norman DAHL,
Consultant,
Ford Foundation,
320 East 43rd Street,
New York, N.Y. 10017,
USA

Guy DARDENNE,
Directeur Générale,
Association pour la Promotion Industrie-Agriculture,
(APRIA),
29, rue du Général Foy,
Paris 8ème,
France

Mohamed DAYA,
Directeur,
Centre d'Etudes Industrielles du Maghreb,
B.P. 235,
Tanger,
Maroc

José P. FERNANDEZ,
Consejo Nacional de Ciencia y Tecnologia,
Insurgentes sur 1677,
Mexico 20 D.F.,
Mexico

Nuno de FIGUEIREDO,
Companhia Progresso do Estado da Guanabara,
Av. Nilo Pecanha 175,
Rio de Janeiro, G.B.,
Brazil

Thomas FOX,
Director, International Program,
Volunteers for International Technical Assistance, Inc.,
(VITA),
College Campus,
Schennectady,
New York 12308,
USA

Michel GERARD,
Secrétaire Général,
Secrétariat des Missions d'Urbanisme et d'Habitat,
11, rue Chardin,
Paris 16ème,
France

José GIRAL, B.,
Consultant,
Universidad Nacional Autonoma de Mexico,
Sierra Ventana No. 678,
Lomas Barrilaco,
Mexico 10 D.F.,
Mexico

Pierre GONOD,
Organisation of American States,
17th Street and Constitution Avenue, N.W.,
Washington D.C. 20006,
USA

Dennis GOULET,
Fellow,
Centre for the Study of Development and Social Change,
1430 Massachusetts Ave. (Harvard Sq.),
Cambridge, MASS. 02138,
USA

Peter HARPER,
c/o Gambles,
40, Lexham Gardens,
London W.8,
United Kingdom

Hans A. HAVEMANN,
Director,
Forschungsinstitut für Internationale Technisch-Wirtschaftliche
Zusammenarbeit,
Postfach 1170,
5100 Aachen,
Federal Republic of Germany

Moises IKONICOFF,
Directeur des Etudes,
Institut d'Etudes du Développement Economique et Social,
(IEDES),
58, Bld. Arago,
Paris 13ème,
France

Pierre JUDET,
Professeur,
Institut de Recherche Economique et de Planification,
Département Industrialisation et Développement,
1, rue du Général Marchand,
38 Grenoble,
France

J. L. KAHN,
Secrétaire Permanent,
Commission de Coopération Technique,
Association Nationale de la Recherche Technique,
(ANRT),
44, rue Copernic,
Paris 16ème,
France

Rainer KRAETSCH,
DED (German Volunteer Service),
151, Friesdorferstrasse,
53 Bonn Bad Godesberg,
Federal Republic of Germany

A. LATHAM-KOENIG,
Secretary General,
Intermediate Technology Development Group,
9, King Street,
Covent Garden,
London, W.C.2.
United Kingdom

Pablo de LORENZI,
Directeur Général,
Centro Nacional de Productividad (CENIP),
Presidencia de la Republica,
Pablo Bermudez 214, piso 10,
Lima,
Peru

S. MRKSA,
Directeur Adjoint,
Institut de Recherche sur les Investissements,
53-55, Ruzveltova,
Belgrade,
Yougoslavie

K. L. NANJAPPA,
Development Commissioner for Small-Scale Industries,
Ministry of Industrial Development and Internal Trade,
Nirman Bhawan,
New Delhi 11,
India

Jean PARENT,
Professeur,
Faculté de Droit et Sciences Economiques Paris I,
3, rue des Chaines,
78 Le Vesinet,
France

Jacques PERRIN,
Professeur,
Institut de Recherche Economique et de Planification,
Département Industrialisation et Développement,
1, rue du Général Marchand,
38 Grenoble,
France

J. P. RUINA,
Professor of Electrical Engineering,
Massachusetts Institute of Technology,
Cambridge, Mass. 02139,
USA

Jorge SABATO,
Director, Department of Metallurgy,
National Commission of Atomic Energy,
Avenida Libergador General San Martin 825,
Buenos Aires,
Argentina

Glenn SCHWEITZER,
Director,
Office of Science and Technology,
AID,
Washington D.C. 20523,
USA

Morisaburo SEKI,
Secretary General,
Asian Productivity Organisation,
Aoyama Daiichi Mansions,
4-14 Akasaka 8-chome,
Minato-ku,
Tokyo 107,
Japan

M.A.M. SHABAAN,
Consultant,
General Organisation for Industrialisation,
4, Moderiet El Tahrir Street,
Garden City,
Cairo,
U.A.R.

Joseph E. STEPANEK,
Director,
Industrial Services and Institutions Division,
UNIDO,
Felderhaus, Rathausplatz 2,
A-1010 Vienna,
Austria

Frances STEWART,
Queen Elizabeth House,
21, St. Giles,
Oxford,
United Kingdom

F. THOUMI,
Economics of Industry Division,
I.B.R.D.,
1818 H. Street, N.W.,
Washington, D.C. 20433,
USA

Simon TEITEL,
(Consultant to the U.S. National Academy of Sciences in
the Study on Appropriate Technology for Development),
Advisor,
Industrial Development and Science and Technology Office
of the Programme Advisor to the President,
Inter-American Development Bank,
Washington, D.C. 20577,
USA

Jean TORCOL,
Directeur,
Institut pour la Technologie et l'Industrialisation des
Produits Agricoles Tropicaux,
B.P. 8881,
Abidjan,
Côte d'Ivoire

P. C. TRUSSELL,
Secretary General,
WAITRO,
3650, Wesbrook Crescent,
Vancouver 8,
Canada

L. NORTON YOUNG,
Director,
Instituto de Investigaciones Technologicas,
Apartados Aereo 7031,
Bogata D.E.,
Colombia

Observers

Guillermo d'AUBAREDE,
Attaché Industriel,
Délégation Permanente de l'Espagne auprès de l'OCDE,
44, Av. d'Iéna,
Paris 16ème,
France

Jacques BEAUMONT,
Professor,
IRFED, 49, rue de la Glacière,
Paris 14ème,
France

Julian ENGEL,
Deputy Director (Special Studies)
Board on Science and Technology for International Development,
National Academy of Sciences,
2101 Constitution Avenue,
Washington D.C. 20418,
USA

Fritz STANGEN,
Ministry of Economic Cooperation,
Bonn,
Federal Republic of Germany

OECD

Ambassador Edwin MARTIN[*]
Chairman, Development Assistance Committee

Rimieri PAULUCCI di CALBOLI[*]
Secrétaire Général Suppléant

Marthe TENZER,
Conseiller Spécial,
Direction de l'Aide au Développement

Ayhan CILINGIROGLU,
Consultant, Technical Cooperation Service

---

[*] Part of the meeting only.

- 231 -

Francois CHESNAIS,
Scientific Affairs Directorate

Giovanni RUFO,
Scientific Affairs Directorate

OECD Development Centre

Paul-Marc HENRY,
Président

Friedrich KAHNERT,
Head of Economic Development Programme and Research

Antoine KHER,
Chef, Direction et Coordination

Mikoto USUI,
Head of Technology and Industrialisation Programme

Martin BROWN,
Technology and Industrialisation Programme

Guy CRESPIN,
Technology and Industrialisation Programme

Antonio DOS SANTOS,
Technology and Industrialisation Programme

Nicole GANIERE,
Technology and Industrialisation Programme

Harald STIER,
Technology and Industrialisation Programme

III. BACKGROUND PAPERS*

Number	Author	Title
1	BEHARI, Bepin	Genesis, Organisation and Action Programme of the Appropriate Technology Cell (Eng. and Fr.)
2	JUDET. P.	Some Studies and Research done by the IREP on Industrialisation Problems (Fr. and Eng.)
3	HAVEMANN, H.A.	The Adaptation of Technology to the Situation in Developing Countries
4	de BANDT, J.	Some Thoughts on the Choice and Adaptation of Techniques in Textile Industries (Fr. and Eng.)
5	RANIS, Gustav	Some Observations on the Economic Framework for Optimum Utilisation of Technology
6.	THOUMI, F.	The International Market of Technology, Direct Foreign Investment Market Structures and Policies for Developed Countries
7	GONOD, Pierre	Recherche d'un Modèle de Mécanisme de Transfer Technologique
7a	GONOD, Pierre	Aperçu Theorique sur le Transfert Technologique et les Notions Connexes
8	OEA (OAS)	Note d'Information sur l'Organisation et l'Etat de Réalisation de Projet Pilote de Transfert de Technologie de l'Organisation des Etats Américains

* Titles not translated into English are only available in French.

9	DAYA, M.	Choix et Adaptation des Technologies dans les Pays en Voie de Développement
10	UNIDO	Guidelines for the Acquisition of Foreign Technology in Developing Countries with Special Reference to Technology Licensing Agreements
11	STEWART, F.	Intermediate Technology: a Definitional Discussion
12	M.I.T.	Technology Adaptation Projects of the Massachusetts Institute of Technology
13	JUDET/PERRIN UNIDO	The Transfer of Technology in an Integrated Programme of Industrial Development
14	PARENT, J.	Les Problèmes des Transferts de Technologie de Branche en Branche et les Effets Multiplicateurs
15	LATHAM-KOENIG, A.	Intermediate Technologies for True Development
16	TORCOL, J.	Le Choix et l'Adaptation des Technologies dans l'Industrie Alimentaire des Pays en Voie de Développement
17	GERARD, M.	Les Conditions d'une Industrialisation dans l'Habitat en Afrique Francophone
18	CARRIERE, D.	Industrial Development in Relation to Industrial Satisfaction (Fr. and Eng.)
19	BEHARI, B.	Terminology Problem - Definition and Development Philosophy
20	BEHARI, B.	Appraisal of Industrial Technology Policies
21	DEVELOPMENT CENTRE	Note on the Council of Europe Recommendation concerning the Establishment of an International Information Centre for Intermediate Technology

22	GIRAL, J.	Development of Appropriate Chemical Technology - A Programme for Mexico
23	FOX, T. (VITA)	Volunteers in Technical Assistance
24	BOON, G. K.	Report on Choice of Technique in Metal Machining Process
25	BOON, G. K.	Employment and Housing
26	IKONICOFF, M.	Le Transfert de Technologie et les Conditions de l'Industrialisation dans le Tiers-Monde
27	UNIDO	In-plant Training Programme for the Utilisation of More Appropriate Technologies - Bandung, Indonesia
28	UNIDO	Selected Bibliography of Documents Prepared by or on Behalf of the United Nations Industrial Development Organisation on the Transfer and Adaptation of Technology
29	HARPER, P.	Soft Technology - A Proposal for Alternatives under Conditions of Crisis
30	GONOD, P.	Un Exemple d'Opération Système: le Programme de Transfert de Technologie de l'OEA
31	COLIN, R.	Politique de Participation et Développement Technologique
32	FERNANDEZ (CONACYT)	The Role of Information in the Transfer of Technology - An Experiment in Mexico
33	JUDET, P. PALLOIX, C.	Grandes Firmes Multinationales et Transfert des Technologies
34	PERRIN, J.	Création de Sociétés d'Engineering dans les Pays en Voie d'Industrialisation comme Moyen de Transfert de Connaissances

35	A.I.D. TA/OST 72-9	Technology and Economics in International Development - Report of a Seminar
36	A.I.D. TA/OST 72-11	Appropriate Technologies for International Development
37	DARDENNE, C.	Le Choix et l'Adaptation de Technologie pour les Pays en Voie de Développement dans le Secteur des Industries Alimentaires
38	NANJAPPA, K. L.	Choice and Adaptation of Technology in Developing Countries (Indian Experience)

SELECTED SOURCES

A. Authors

BARANSON - Industrial Technologies for Developing Economies,
    Praeger, 1969.

CAILLOT Robert - "L'Enquete-Participation à l'Économie et Human-
    isme" in Cahier de l'Institut Canadien d'Education des Adultes,
    No. 3 (February 1967).
- "Une Connaissance Engagée : L'Enquete-Participation" in Options
    Humanistes, (Paris: Les Editions Ouvr. 1968).

COMMONER Barry - The Closing Circle, Cape, 1972.

DIDIJER S. - "National R and D Policy as a Social Innovation", in
    Management of Research and Development, OECD, Paris 1972.

ELLUL J. - The Technological Society (Knopf, 1964).

ENOS John L. - The Rate and Direction of Inventive Activity,
    Princeton University Press, 1962.

FERNE G. - "In Search of a Policy" in Research System, Vol.I
    (France, Germany, U.K.), OECD 1972.

GALBRAITH D. - The New Industrial Estate, Hamish, Hamilton, 1967.

HARPER P. and ERIKSSON B. - "Alternative Technology : A Guide to
    Sources and Contacts", Undercurrents No. 3 (1972), 34, Cholmley
    Gardens, Aldred Road, London, N.W.6.

HAWTHORNE Edward P. - Report of OECD Seminar in Istambul 5-9 Oct.
    1970: The Transfer of Technology, OECD, Paris 1971.
- Innovation-oriented Management, Paper submitted to the CIOS
    World Congress, Munich, 1972.

ISARD W., SCHOOLER E.W. and VIETORICZ T. - Industrial Complex
    Analysis and Regional Development, MIT Press Cambridge, 1959.

JANTSCH E. - "From Forecasting and Planning to Policy Science" in Management of Research and Development.

JUDET, PERRIN and TIBERGEIN - L'Engineering (Rapport Provisoire) IREP, Université des Sciences Sociales de Grenoble, May 1970.

JUDET and PERRIN - Planification des Industries Mécaniques et Situation de l'Engineering en Hongrie, November, December, 1970.

KINDLEBERGER C.P. - American Business Abroad: Six Lectures on Direct Investment, New Haven and London, 1969.

KRAUCH Helmut - Papers delivered at CSDI (Santa Barbara, California): "Experiments, Experience and Planning"; "Public Control of Government Planning"; "Can Reality be Simulated?".

MANNE A.S. and MARKOWITZ H.M. ed. - Studies in Process Analysis, Economywide Production Capabilities, Cowles Foundation, Monograph No.18, John Wiley and Sons Inc., New York, 1961.

MARCUSE Herbert - One-Dimensional Man, Sphere, London, 1969.

McDERMOTT John - "Technology, the Opiate of the Intellectuals" New York Review of Books 13, (2), 1969.

MITSUI I.D.I. - Association for Machinery Promotion (Centre for New Machine System), Analysis of the Japanese Industrial Structure from the Information-Knowledge Intensity Viewpoint, Tokyo, May 1972 (in Japanese).

MUMFORD Lewis - The Pentagon of Power, Harcourt, Brace and Jovanovich, 1970.

PACK Howard - "The Use of Labour Intensive Techniques in Kenyan Industry" in Technology and Economics in International Development, AID, Washington D.C., May 1972.

PERRIN - L'Engineering en Roumanie, April 1972.
- Place et Fonction de l'Ingenierie dans le Système Industriel Français. March, 1973.

RANIS G. - "Some Observations on the Economic Framework for Optimum LDC Utilisation of Technology" in Economic Growth Centre Discussion Paper No.152, Yale University.

RAVETZ J.R. - Scientific Knowledge and its Social Problems, Oxford University Press, 1971.

ROBERTS and PERRIN - Engineering en Inde, November 1970.

ROBERTS - Engineering en Inde, Tome II, March 1972.

ROSENBERG Nathan - "Factors Affecting the Diffusion of Technology" in Exploration in Economic History, Autumn 1972, Vol. 10, No.1.

ROSZAK Theodore - The Making of a Counter-Culture, Faber, 1969.

SCHWEITZER Glenn - "Towards a Methodology for Assessing the Impact of Technology in Developing Countries", in Technology and Economics in International Development, AID, Washington, D.C., May 1972.

SIGURDSSON Jon - "Rural Industrialisation in China", Science Policy Research Unit, University of Sussex, Brighton, 1972.

STREETEN Paul - "Costs and Benefits of Multinational Enterprises in Less Developed Countries" in John H. Dunning, ed. The Multinational Enterprise, George Allen and Unwin, London, 1971.

TURKKAM and ERDEMLI - Engineering en Turquie, March 1971.

TURKKAM - Engineering au Japon, July 1972.

VALLURI S.R. - "Mobilisation of National Resources and Planning of Industrial Research and Development", UNIDO, ID/WG.132/10, Vienna, October 1972.

VIETORICZ Thomas - "Programming Data Summary for the Chemical Industry", Industrialisation and Productivity Bulletin 10, U.N., New Yori, 1966.

WELLS L.T. Jr. - "Economic Man and Engineering Man: Choice of Technology in a Low Wage Country" in Economic Development Report, Harvard Development Advisory Service, Cambridge, Mass., Autumn 1972.

B.   National and International Organisations

ILO - Scope, Approach and Content of Research-Oriented Activities of the World Employment Programme, Geneva 1972.

INSEE - Data Banks for Development: Proceedings of the International Expert Meeting, St. Maxim, 24-28 May, 1971, Observatoire Economique Mediterraneen, Marseille.

UNACAST - <u>Record of the 17th Session</u>, 23 October-1 November, 1972.

UNCTAD - "<u>Technology Transfer</u>", Report by the Secretariat, TD/106,
    10 November, 1972.

UNESCO - <u>A Methodology for Planning Technological Development</u>,
    Report by Arthur D. Little Inc. and Hetrick Associates Inc.,
    Paris, September 1970.

UNIDO - <u>The Transfer of Technology in an Integrate Programme of
    Industrial Development</u>, IPPD.53, Vienna, 15 October, 1971.

US AID - <u>Technology and Economics in International Development</u>
    Report of the Seminar held in Washington D.C. on 23 May, 1972,
    Office of Science and Technology (TA/OST 72-9).

- "Multinational Corporations and Adaptive Research for Developing
    Countries" in <u>Appropriate Technologies for International Devel-
    opment: Preliminary Survey of Research Activities</u>, Washington,
    D.C., September 1972.

OECD PUBLICATIONS
2, rue André-Pascal, 75775 Paris Cedex 16
———
No. 32.743 1974

PRINTED IN FRANCE